INTERNATIO
REGIONAL DEVE

Global growth slows while inflation accelerates

- The global economy faces numerous challenges including broadening inflation, slowing growth in the People's Republic of China (PRC), and the persisting impacts of the Russian invasion of Ukraine and the shock from the coronavirus disease (COVID-19) pandemic. In response to inflation, the United States (US) is undertaking rapid monetary tightening to cool domestic demand and prompting many other economies to follow its pace. Europe is experiencing a severe energy crisis that is eroding living standards and depressing economic activity. The International Monetary Fund forecasts global growth of 3.2% in 2022 and 2.7% in 2023, the weakest since 2001 barring the global financial crisis and the initial phase of the COVID-19 pandemic. Downward risks to the outlook are excessive monetary tightening, leading to risk of debt distress among developing economies, further international commodity price shocks exacerbating inflation and depressing output, financial and real economy spillovers from a possible worsening of the PRC property crisis, and geopolitical fragmentation following the Russian invasion of Ukraine and the US-PRC trade tensions impeding trade and capital flows.

- Developing Asia is seen growing by 4.2% in 2022 and 4.7% in 2023 as its recovery continues, but the outlook has worsened relative to the *Asian Development Outlook 2022* largely because of a slowdown in the PRC even as inflation is rising. COVID-19 lockdowns and a slump in the property sector in the PRC weigh on both domestic and global economic activities. A sharp deceleration in global growth, stronger-than-expected monetary policy tightening in advanced economies, an escalation in the Russian invasion of Ukraine, a deeper-than-expected deceleration in the PRC, and negative pandemic developments could all dent developing Asia's growth over the forecast horizon.

- In the Pacific, faster growth is expected relative to the *Asian Development Outlook 2022* with economic activity in the subregion expanding by 5.3% this year. The brighter outlook is mainly because of a stronger-than-expected recovery in tourism in Fiji and an upward adjustment to the growth forecast for Papua New Guinea owing to a recovery in the minerals sector and election-related spending. The adjustment in the subregional forecast masks downward revisions in the outlook for several economies, however: Tonga, because the impact of the volcanic eruption in January 2022 has been more severe than expected; Palau, owing to a slower recovery in tourism; and the Marshall Islands, Samoa, and Solomon Islands, all affected by COVID-19 restrictions. The growth outlook for 2023 is revised downward to 4.8% from 5.4%, as the recovery in Fiji stabilizes following the stronger-than-anticipated tourism performance in 2022. Inflation is forecast to rise steeply as international prices remain elevated. Smaller island economies account for the biggest upward adjustments with their narrow economic bases and high import dependency, making them particularly sensitive to international price movements.

- After contracting for two consecutive quarters over the first half of 2022, the US economy grew by a stronger-than-expected 2.9% annualized pace in the third quarter. The return to growth followed annualized declines of 1.6% in the first quarter and 0.6% in the second quarter that were attributed to the lingering impacts of the pandemic on consumption and investment, as well as reduced public spending. High inflation has emerged as the primary concern,

GDP Growth (%, annual)

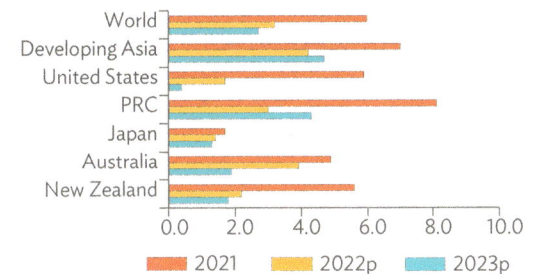

ADB = Asian Development Bank, GDP = gross domestic product, p = projection, PRC = People's Republic of China.

Notes: Developing Asia and Pacific developing member countries as defined by ADB. Figures are based on ADB estimates except for world gross domestic product growth.

Sources: Asian Development Outlook database (accessed 6 December 2022); and International Monetary Fund. 2022. *World Economic Outlook: Countering the Cost-of-Living Crisis.* Washington, DC (October).

GDP Growth in Developing Asia (%, annual)

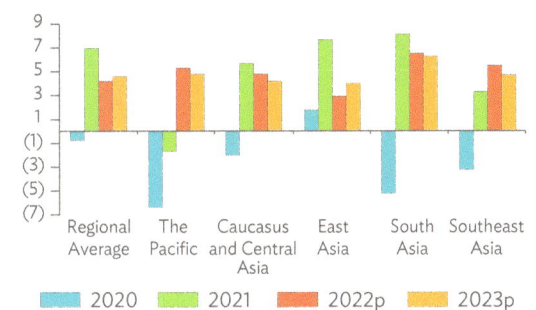

( ) = negative, GDP = gross domestic product, p = projection.
Source: Asian Development Outlook database (accessed 6 December 2022).

COVID-19 Vaccination Coverage in the Pacific (% of total population)

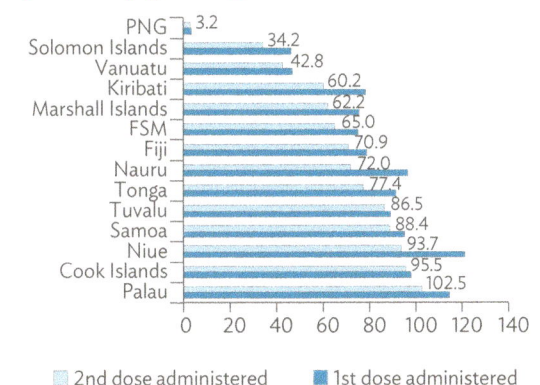

COVID-19 = coronavirus disease, FSM = Federated States of Micronesia, PNG = Papua New Guinea, RMI = Republic of the Marshall Islands.

Note: Data as of 21 November 2022.

Source: ADB estimates using data from Pacific Data Hub. COVID-19 vaccination (accessed 25 November 2022).

COVID-19 Cases in the Pacific

	Total Cases	Active Cases	Total Deaths	Total Cases /1,000 Population
Fiji	68,375	1,057	878	75.17
PNG	45,819	1,169	668	4.93
Solomon Islands	24,575	–	153	34.08
FSM	22,203	–	55	189.01
Tonga	16,182	532	12	149.66
Samoa	15,946	14,312	29	79.30
Marshall Islands	15,501	112	17	258.35
Vanuatu	11,952	1	14	37.15
Cook Islands	6,389	4	1	363.07
Palau	5,684	101	7	311.13
Nauru	4,621	11	1	421.55
Kiribati	3,430	714	13	27.85
Tuvalu	2,805	2,805	–	232.07
Niue	107	16	–	64.93
World	644,898,272	14,595,877	6,632,769	82.73

– = none, COVID-19 = coronavirus disease, FSM = Federated States of Micronesia, PNG = Papua New Guinea.

Notes: Data as of 25 November 2022.

Sources: Worldometer. Worldometer COVID-19 Data and Population (accessed 25 November 2022); and authors' calculations.

Average Spot Price of Brent Crude Oil
(monthly, $/barrel)

Source: World Bank. 2022. *World Bank Commodity Price Data (Pink Sheet)*.

however, affecting consumer confidence and prompting aggressive monetary tightening by the US Federal Reserve. Growth in US is expected to weaken to 1.7% for the full year and further slow to 0.4% in 2023. Gross domestic product (GDP) growth in the third quarter was bolstered by a narrowing trade deficit and increases in consumer spending, nonresidential fixed investment, and government spending.

- While growth in the rest of Developing Asia has remained strong, economic activity has significantly slowed in the PRC. After expanding by 2.5% in the first half of 2022, GDP growth picked up to 3.9% in the third quarter mainly because of robust investment and export growth. While consumption spending and trade continue to grow, both have slowed since the start of the year and a prolonged slump is seen in the property sector. The PRC's economic expansion is forecast to slow to 3.0% in 2022 primarily because of COVID-19-related lockdowns, problems in its property sector, and weaker external demand. Growth is expected to increase to 4.3% in 2023 as the impact of COVID-19 wanes. However, challenges to the growth outlook include a deteriorating property market, which has potential ramifications for the financial system; international supply chain disruptions; and a greater-than-expected reduction in external demand.

- Following the lifting of COVID-19 mobility restrictions, holiday-related spending on semi-durable goods and services, and improved business investment, GDP growth in Japan recovered robustly in the second quarter of 2022. While the economy grew further by 1.8% year-on-year in the third quarter, it declined on a quarterly basis. Indicating a reversal in the momentum of economic activity. The outlook is constrained by continuing impacts of supply chain disruptions on exports, and of rising inflation on consumer spending exacerbated by a depreciating yen. GDP is expected to grow by 1.4% in 2022 and 1.3% in 2023. Upside risks to the outlook include the restart of nuclear power plants, normalization of international travel, and an upcoming fiscal package. The main downside risk would be a failure by the Bank of Japan to appropriately time the exit from its current accommodative monetary policy stance as price pressures accelerate.

- Australia sustained its economic growth in the second quarter of 2022 with seasonally adjusted GDP growing by 0.9% amid increased consumer spending and strong exports. Spending on travel-related items such as transport, hotels, and restaurants continued to drive household spending—which accelerated to 2.2% as COVID-19 movement restrictions eased—but it remains below pre-pandemic levels. Exports posted the strongest quarterly performance since the quarter of September 2000, contributing 1.1 percentage points to GDP growth largely because of higher global commodity prices for mineral and agricultural commodities. Domestically, the annual figure of its consumer price index accelerated to 6.1% in the June 2022 quarter with construction of new dwellings and fuel as the main drivers. FocusEconomics projects the economy to grow by 3.9% in 2022 and 1.9% in 2023.

- New Zealand's economy bounced back in the second quarter of 2022 as relaxation of COVID-19 restrictions contributed to a revival of tourism. The seasonally adjusted GDP for the quarter of June 2022 grew by 1.7%, a reversal of the previous quarter's contraction. Both residents and international tourists recorded higher spending on transport, accommodation, restaurants, and recreational activities. Exports increased by 20.5% in the same quarter, dominated by a 60.7% jump in exports of services. However, household spending on both durable and nondurable goods declined, pulling overall private consumption expenditure down by 3.1%. Annual inflation in the June 2022 quarter surged to a 32-year high of 7.3%. With

Food Prices
(January 2020 = 100)

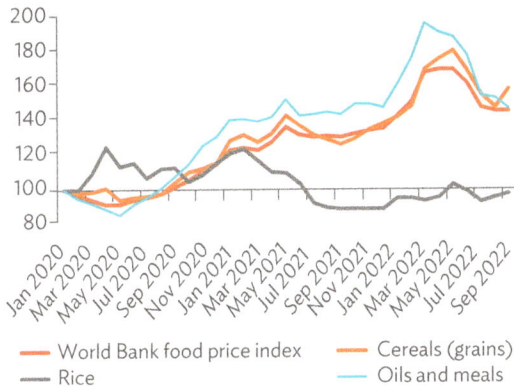

- World Bank food price index
- Rice
- Cereals (grains)
- Oils and meals

Sources: ADB calculations using data from World Bank. 2022. *Commodity Markets Outlook: Pandemic, war, recession: Drivers of aluminum and copper prices, October 2022.* Washington, DC; and World Bank. 2022. *World Bank Commodity Price Data (Pink Sheet)* (accessed 28 October 2022).

Prices of Export Commodities
(January 2020 = 100)

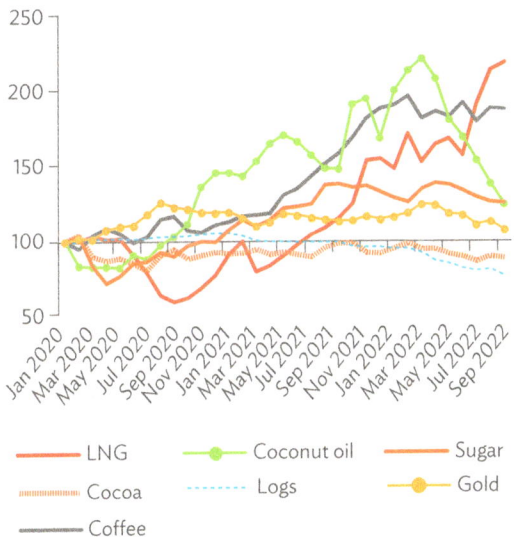

- LNG
- Cocoa
- Coffee
- Coconut oil
- Logs
- Sugar
- Gold

LNG = liquefied natural gas.

Sources: ADB calculations using data from World Bank. 2022. *Commodity Markets Outlook: Pandemic, war, recession: Drivers of aluminum and copper prices, October 2022.* Washington, DC; and World Bank. 2022. *World Bank Commodity Price Data (Pink Sheet)* (accessed 28 October 2022).

the Reserve Bank of New Zealand adopting a hawkish stance on inflation, the pace of economic growth is expected to slow this year. FocusEconomics projects the economy to grow by 2.2% this year and 1.8% in 2023.

Uncertainties weigh on global commodity prices

- The price of Brent crude oil recorded a sharp decline in the third quarter of 2022 with its quarterly price average 12.0% lower than in the previous quarter. This reflected a slowdown in global growth and concerns about a worldwide recession. Meanwhile global oil production has gone up by 2.0% this quarter and has now returned to its pre-pandemic level. Brent crude oil is still expected to post an average price of $100 per barrel in 2022, 42.0% higher than in 2021, before declining in the next 2 years.

- Agricultural commodity prices fell in the third quarter of 2022 after surging in the previous quarter. Increased global food supply, driven by larger-than-expected production of edible oils and oilseeds and shipments of Ukrainian grain to global markets, as well as weakening global growth prospects have pulled down food prices by 12.3%. Grain prices declined because of a United Nations-brokered deal which facilitated grain exports from Ukraine as well as higher wheat production by key exporters. For the whole year, the food price index is projected to increase by 17.9% then decline by 6.2% in 2023.

- In contrast, natural gas prices soared, particularly in Europe, still driven by the ongoing Russian invasion of Ukraine. Natural gas prices in Europe have shot up by 90.1% in the third quarter of 2022 because of the aggressive importation of liquefied natural gas (LNG) by several European countries to replenish their inventories after the reduced flows from the Russian Federation in the second quarter of 2022. Meanwhile, LNG contract prices in Japan increased by 21.5% in the third quarter compared to the previous quarter. The full-year price forecast for LNG prices is expected to soar 70.4% in 2022 but will fall in the next 2 succeeding years as major importers like Japan and the Republic of Korea diversify away from natural gas. Gold prices declined by 7.8% in the third quarter of 2022 considering the successive policy rate increases implemented by the US Federal Reserve and the subsequent appreciation of the US dollar. With the US Federal Reserve's hawkish policy expected to continue well into 2023, gold prices are expected to continue to decline. For other Pacific major export commodities, prices of coffee and coconut oil are expected to rise sharply while cocoa and log prices are expected to fall in 2022. Sugar prices are expected to remain flat.

Uneven recovery in tourism to the Pacific

- With all South Pacific destinations having reopened their borders to international tourists by the third quarter of 2022, the nascent recovery from the start of the year has further consolidated, boosted by continuing strong outbound tourism from Australia and New Zealand. During January–August 2022, the total number of Australian tourists bound for Fiji reached 84% of pre-pandemic levels. A similarly rapid pace of recovery is observed in tourism to the Cook Islands from New Zealand. The flow of tourists from New Zealand to Fiji likewise picked up in recent months and now stands at more than half of pre-pandemic numbers. Vanuatu, which opened its borders in July 2022, has gradually reclaimed about 10%–11% of its usual tourist numbers from both Australia and New Zealand. More modest gains have been observed in Samoa (4%–5% of pre-pandemic levels) and Tonga (3%–9%), which both reopened in August 2022.

Outbound Tourism from Major Source Markets
(relative to pre–COVID-19 pandemic levels, monthly)

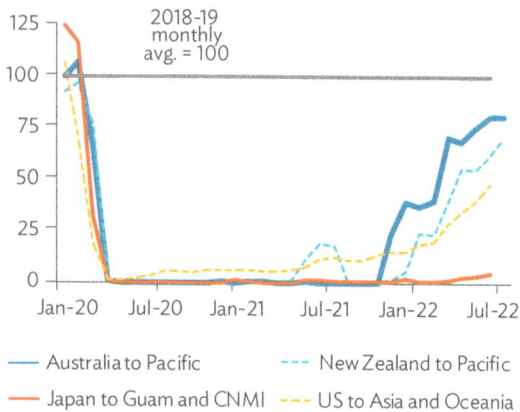

- Australia to Pacific
- New Zealand to Pacific
- Japan to Guam and CNMI
- US to Asia and Oceania

avg. = average, COVID-19 = coronavirus disease,
CNMI = Commonwealth of the Northern Mariana Islands,
US = United States.

Sources: Australian Bureau of Statistics, Japan Tourism Marketing Co., Statistics New Zealand, and US Department of Commerce International Trade Administration.

Tourist Departures Bound for Pacific Destinations
('000 persons, January–August totals)

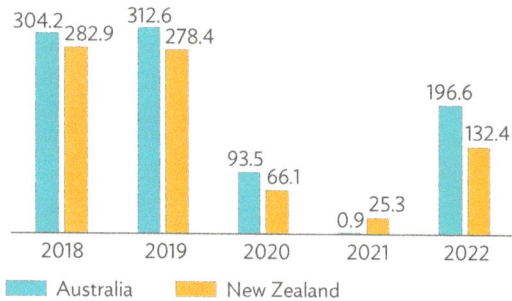

- Australia
- New Zealand

Sources: Australian Bureau of Statistics and Statistics New Zealand.

Lead authors: Remrick Patagan, Noel Del Castillo, and Rommel Rabanal.

- By contrast, despite being open to international tourists since mid-2021, visitor arrivals in Palau have remained at only about 14% of pre-pandemic levels by September 2022. This is largely driven by a more conservative approach to resuming international tourism by Palau's main source markets in East Asia. For example, even with restored flight links, tourism from Japan—Palau's second-largest source of tourists—to neighboring Guam and the Commonwealth of the Northern Mariana Islands remains at less than 5% of pre-pandemic levels as of July 2022. Outbound tourism from the United States (Palau's fifth largest source market) to Asia and Oceania has also not recovered at the same pace as Australia and New Zealand that has benefited South Pacific destinations. This suggests that, beyond restoring flight links, Palau will need innovative marketing and recovery strategies to reclaim lost ground, particularly considering likely intense competition from neighboring destinations in Asia in coming months and years.

Poverty and vulnerability, including from climate change, are increasing in the Pacific. However, traditional social protection systems are coming under stress from rising urbanization, food scarcity, and migration, even as formal systems remain generally underdeveloped in the subregion. Social protection comprises a set of policies and programs that are designed to reduce poverty and vulnerability by promoting efficient labor markets, diminishing people's exposure to risks, and enhancing their capacity to protect themselves against hazards and/or interruption and/or loss of income. This falls into three broad categories: social insurance, social assistance, and labor market programs.

Over the past 2 years, social protection in the Pacific was largely skewed toward mitigating the impacts of the coronavirus disease (COVID-19) pandemic through measures such as unemployment assistance, in-kind support, temporary jobs, and utility subsidies. Assistance from development partners supported many of these efforts, which eased some of the pressure on the limited fiscal resources of the Pacific economies. After learning to live with COVID-19, the subregion must now return its attention to long-standing social development concerns, with renewed focus on strengthening social safety nets to help build resilience to further shocks from climate change, disasters, and possible health emergencies. However, socioeconomic scarring and depleted resources arising from the pandemic have complicated the efforts to sustain social protection in this "new normal."

COUNTRY ECONOMIC ISSUES

Social protection and sustainability: A case study of the Cook Islands and Niue

Lead authors: Lily-Anne Homasi and Isoa Wainiqolo

The Cook Islands has one of the most established and generous social protection systems in the Pacific. The Cook Islands Welfare Act 1989 and Welfare Amendment Act 2014 mandate the provision of social welfare benefits. Currently, there are 10 types of social welfare benefits and the government introduced additional support for workers, businesses, families, the elderly, and children to cope with the coronavirus disease (COVID-19) pandemic. Niue also has a generous social protection system that is guided by its Pension and Benefits Act 1991. Apart from the superannuation scheme for public sector workers, there are six social assistance schemes, namely child allowance, newborn infant grant, Niue pension, welfare disability benefit, welfare hardship benefit, and funeral assistance.

This article discusses the social protection systems of Cook Islands and Niue and their fiscal impacts, and draws lessons to strengthen further the sustainability of social protection programs in these economies. Lessons could be useful for neighboring countries as well.

OVERVIEW OF SOCIAL PROTECTION SYSTEMS

Cook Islands. Social protection is enshrined in the Cook Islands 1965 Constitution, which reflects the highest level of commitment by a nation to safeguard the most vulnerable members of its society. The programs are also guided by the 1989 Welfare Act and 2014 Welfare Amendment Act, and the country's *Economic Development Strategy 2030—Objective 1: Improving equity and access for all*. Besides the broader education and health support, there are two main types of social protection programs afforded to Cook Islanders: the traditional social welfare schemes and social insurance. The Ministry of Internal Affairs leads on the social welfare and employment and

training schemes, while the Cook Islands National Superannuation Fund covers social insurance (Table 1).

Prior to the pandemic, the government's expenditure on social protection was NZ$20.8 million in fiscal year 2018 (FY2018, ended 30 June 2018) (equivalent to 4.0% of gross domestic product [GDP]) up from NZ$13.9 million in FY2012 (3.7% of GDP). Social assistance accounted for over 90% of social protection spending, with old age allowance having the largest share.

For a small island nation with capacity constraints, the Cook Islands mobilized a lot for its affected citizens. For instance, during the COVID-19 pandemic, the government increased its resourcing for social protection as part of its response by 13.5% from FY2018 levels to NZ$23.6 million, equivalent to 5.5% of GDP in FY2022. This was 10.5% of the government's operating expenditure in FY2022, which helped vulnerable people meet their basic needs.

As part of its fiscal stimulus package, the government produced an Economic Response Plan that included numerous social protection initiatives. A wage subsidy, training subsidy, "Fees Free" initiative, unemployment benefit, school closure benefit, electricity discount, emergency hardship fund, and one-off payment to vulnerable people (mainly those who lost their jobs during border closures) were put in place and reduced much of the negative socioeconomic impacts felt by individuals and businesses.

In collaboration with several government agencies, the Ministry of Internal Affairs utilized the existing social assistance system to roll out support quickly for school children to continue their education during closures and welfare recipients, and manage the unemployment benefit, employment services, and the hardship fund (Table 2). The Cook Islands National Superannuation Fund worked with the Ministry of Finance and Economic Management to manage the wage subsidy. Table 2 presents the amounts spent on the initiatives, with the wage subsidy being by far the largest

Table 1: Social Protection Programs in the Cook Islands

No.	Category	Description
1	Social welfare assistance	
	(i) Old age pensions	Assists elderly who are in retirement. NZ$500/month: (60–69 years old). NZ$700/month: (70+ years)
	(ii) Newborn allowance	For newborns in need of accessories. NZ$1,000 (one-off payment)
	(iii) Child benefit	Assist parents/guardians with education costs. NZ$100/month (0–16 years)
	(iv) Infirm benefit	Unemployed due to a disability. NZ$200/month (16 years and over)
	(v) Destitute benefit	Hardship allowance for those not able to support themselves financially. NZ$200/month (18 years and over)
	(vi) Caregivers allowance	For those caring for the elderly. NZ$200/month (18 years and over)
	(vii) Funeral allowance	To assist families with funeral expenses. NZ$2,400 for pensioners; NZ$1,200 for infirm and destitute beneficiary; and NZ$600 for child
	(viii) Power subsidy	To assist vulnerable Cook Islanders with utilities bill. NZ$66 paid quarterly to the utility
	(ix) Christmas bonus	To assist families during festive season. All eligible beneficiaries receive NZ$50 at the end of the year
	(x) Maternity leave payout	For Cook Islanders only
2	Social insurance Superannuation	For public servants and voluntary members who may wish to save for their retirement
3	Labor market programs Education and skills training	Free public education (5–15 years old) and training

Source: Government of the Cook Islands, Ministry of Internal Affairs. Forms, Fact Sheets & Policies.

Table 2: Economic Response Plan Expenditure and Beneficiaries by Initiative, April 2020–June 2021

Initiative	Amount of Support Provided	Amount and Frequency	Number of Beneficiaries
Wage subsidy for formal workers	NZ$55,754,013	NZ$160–NZ$320 per week	3,563 individuals 411 businesses
Sole trader grant for businesses	NZ$3,867,500	NZ$3,000 paid up to five instances	356 businesses
One-off payment for social welfare beneficiaries	NZ$868,400	NZ$400 one off	2,171 individuals
Unemployment benefit for affected workers	NZ$390,884	NZ$150–NZ$266 per week	299 individuals
School closure support for children and parents/caregivers	NZ$474,200	NZ$100 one off	4,742 individuals
Emergency hardship fund for vulnerable people	NZ$30,101	NZ$150–NZ$250 per week	28 individuals

Notes:

1. These figures are as of 15 December 2021.

2. Gender disaggregated data are not available. The number of beneficiaries of the wage subsidy, training subsidy, and sole trader grant varies from month to month. For these initiatives, the highest number of monthly beneficiaries has been included.

Sources: Government of the Cook Islands, Ministry of Finance and Economic Management and Ministry of Internal Affairs.

expenditure that reached 3,563 people, while only 28 received support through the emergency hardship fund. The government also provided in-kind assistance, including seedlings and agricultural materials. The government, which employs a significant proportion of the population, also maintained the public servant payroll at full pay with no pandemic-related redundancies.

Sustaining such programs during economic downturns can be challenging, and it affected the government's fiscal outlook and recovery efforts.

Niue. Niue's social protection programs are aligned with the Pension and Benefits Act 1991, the Child Allowance Act (1955), and the National Strategic Plan 2026–2026 which emphasizes the government's intention to build opportunities for the people of Niue to lead healthy, prosperous lives while protecting the environment and creating wealth.

Social protection programs in Niue can be classified into three categories: social insurance, social assistance, and labor market programs. Social insurance includes the superannuation scheme which makes up 14.3% of total social protection spending in 2018 (Table 3). Social assistance makes up the bulk of social protection in Niue (85.6% of social protection spending) and includes a pension scheme, child welfare, newborn infant grant, welfare disability benefit, funeral, special assistance, and welfare hardship benefit.

The government's superannuation program covers public sector employees only. Ninety-two percent of social protection expenditure benefits the 20% of the population aged 60 and above. This creates fiscal risks as Niue has an aging population. Employees in the private sector are not privy to the superannuation scheme and are likely to rely on government pension when they retire. Apart from the social insurance offered by the superannuation fund and free health services with easy access to medical referral to New Zealand, Niue does not have workplace injury-related protection for loss of income or health.

School enrollment is free and compulsory for children aged 5–16 years old. Tertiary scholarships are available for further studies in New Zealand or elsewhere. Under the Child Allowance Act (1955), NZ$85 per fortnight per eligible child is provided from birth until the child reaches 18 years of age. The government also issues a one-off newborn infant grant of NZ$2,000 disbursed in four fortnightly payments to help support the needs of the newborn.

The welfare disability cash transfer of NZ$150–NZ$180 per fortnight helps those living with a disability until they find full employment. The government also offers a welfare hardship benefit of NZ$100–NZ$150 to those who meet certain criteria such as loss of employment and time spent as a care provider.

The economically active age group (15–59 years old) decreased from 57% of the total population in 2011 to 53% in 2017. However, the Youth Employment Scheme, which is supported by the United Nations Development Fund, is an innovative idea that can be used as a model for other Pacific island countries. This program provides an avenue for senior high school students to experience a working environment and its usual demands, and help them make career choices. The Chamber of Commerce also runs a separate Young Entrepreneurship Program that targets year 5 and year 6 students at Niue Primary School. Both programs aim to support labor market matching through skills training and on-the-job exposure.

FISCAL RISKS

While social protection measures in the Cook Islands and Niue compare favorably with other Pacific economies, the associated financial risks for continuing such programs in the long term need to be considered.

In the Cook Islands, the government's fiscal deficit reached the equivalent of 20.9% of GDP in FY2021 compared to surpluses registered prior to the pandemic. The various programs under the Economic Response Plan drove this spending. The government's FY2023 budget reported that in FY2022, the old age and special allowance accounted for 55.2% of social protection spending and the family and child allowance accounted for 31.8%. Further, the impact of COVID-19 has intensified and drawn attention to fiscal implications of existing social inequities in the Cook Islands. Despite the enormous support provided, some of the response measures were inadequate. Preliminary findings of a Ministry of Internal Affairs *Socio-Economic Survey on COVID-19-related Vulnerabilities and Perceptions* (2020) indicate that a small proportion of the population faces genuine hardship. Of the 119 households surveyed, which is made up of people already receiving social welfare benefits, 16.8% did not have access to adequate food supply and 18.0% were struggling to meet their basic needs. With emerging fiscal risks including liquidity issues experienced by the country, it is critical to revisit the legislative, budgetary, and monitoring and evaluation frameworks to ensure that social protection programs are sustainable.

In Niue's case, the government has reported fiscal deficits equivalent to 7.3% of GDP in FY2021 (ended 30 June 2021) and 13.3% of GDP in FY2022. The fiscal deficit is projected to widen to 21.4% of GDP in FY2023. Current baseline projections are for similar ratios over the next 2 fiscal years. As per recent Pacific Community population estimates, a total of 324 were qualified for the old age schemes in 2018, and current projections show similar demand numbers until at least 2030. The need for child support is 50% higher. Social protection expenditure, equivalent to 8.4% of GDP in 2018, is thus likely to remain at high levels.

Table 3: Distribution of Social Protection Expenditures in Niue, 2018

Social Protection Category	% Share to Total Social Protection Spending	% Share to GDP
Social insurance		
- Superannuation	14.3	1.2
Social assistance	85.6	7.2
- Pension	77.2	6.5
- Child welfare	3.7	0.3
- Newborn infant grant	1.6	0.2
- Welfare disability benefit	1.1	0.1
- Funeral assistance and special assistance	1.4	0.1
- Welfare hardship benefit	0.6	0.1
Labor market programs	0.1	0.0
- Skills development and training		
Total	100.0	8.4

GDP = gross domestic product.
Source: Asian Development Bank. Forthcoming. *Technical Assistance to Niue for the Social Protection Indicator 2018*. Manila.

POLICY SUGGESTIONS

The fiscal pressures that the two economies face post-COVID-19 are likely to persist for a while as premature withdrawal of policies may be counterproductive. The need for social protection is also likely to remain but requires improved targeting. At a micro level, improved data collection can help focus social protection support. This can include collecting data such as sex, age, disability, and even medical conditions to aid budgeting for relevant support in the future. Once support is carried out, there is also a need for a monitoring and evaluation framework to check on the effectiveness of delivery and inform future activities. There may also be room to expand support through unemployment benefits, but this should be carefully considered so as not to provide further drain on public finances. A proper disability study may be needed also to better inform their needs.

A social protection policy with clearly set objectives may be warranted in the Cook Islands to guide and operationalize the intent of the different programs under the Welfare Act. In terms of the allocation of social protection beneficiaries across age groups, the share of the young and middle-aged working population may need to be improved. The attraction of the working-age populace moving to New Zealand, given Niue's dual citizenship privileges, may be compensated to some extent if similar incentives are provided in the country. This may also involve the provision of superannuation options for private sector employees in close consultation with the private sector. The government also needs to refocus elements of grant support to address social protection and ease the future fiscal burden of such initiatives.

References

Asian Development Bank. Forthcoming. *Technical Assistance to Niue for the Social Protection Indicator 2018.* Manila.

Beazley, R., H. Gorman, S. Santriana, and J. Attenborough. 2021. *Social protection responses to the COVID-19 pandemic in the Pacific: A tipping point for the sector?*

Government of the Cook Islands, Ministry of Internal Affairs. 2020. *Socio-Economic Survey on COVID-19-related Vulnerabilities and Perceptions.* Rarotonga.

Government of the Cook Islands. 2021. *Economic Development Strategy 2030.* Rarotonga.

Government of the Cook Islands, Ministry of Finance and Economic Management. 2022. *Budget Estimates 2022/23: Book 1 – Appropriation Estimates and Commentary.* Rarotonga.

Government of the Cook Islands, Ministry of Internal Affairs. Forms, Fact Sheets & Policies.

Pacific Community. Pacific Data Hub (accessed 21 November 2022).

United Nations Development Fund. 2022. *YES! to preparing youths for the workforce in Niue.*

Accelerating Fiji's recovery: Opportunities to expand youth employment and reduce brain drain

Lead authors: Noel Del Castillo and Isoa Wainiqolo

Fiji, like other economies that are dependent on tourism, suffered when the COVID-19 pandemic forced the closure of borders and the imposition of movement restrictions. With the economic contraction, the closure of many tourism-related businesses dealt a huge blow to workers who lost their jobs and primary source of livelihood. The impact was particularly severe for younger workers, who are mostly employed in those sectors that were hit hardest by the pandemic. The youth unemployment is estimated to have grown to between 29.8% and 36.8% in 2020 (ILO and ADB 2020).[1]

Another challenge facing Fiji has been a steady increase in the emigration of skilled labor, particularly to Australia, New Zealand, and the United States. As of mid-2019, more than 222,000 Fiji-born people resided abroad, equivalent to a quarter of Fiji's population, with 95% living in Australia, Canada, New Zealand, or the United States (US) (International Organization for Migration 2020). In the first 10 months of 2022, more Fiji citizens departed Fiji for emigration and employment purposes in Australia and the US than annual figures since 2016.[2] A positive effect of emigration has been to boost remittances which play a critical role in stabilizing Fiji's external position and providing much needed cash to Fijians during the pandemic. Remittances are likely to continue to grow over the medium term, yet the potential for brain drain to exacerbate skills gaps is an emerging concern.

As Fiji's strong economic rebound continues, these headwinds need to be addressed to sustain the pace of its recovery. Achieving this will require targeted labor market strategies, such as long-term training programs, to expand the supply and skills of workers and mitigate the problem of brain drain.

YOUTH UNEMPLOYMENT

The December 2019 issue of the *Pacific Economic Monitor* discussed the challenges for creating sufficient youth employment opportunities in Fiji and its importance for raising productivity to sustain growth momentum (Wainiqolo 2019). Given the wide-ranging impact that the COVID-19 pandemic brought, these challenges have grown.

Movement restrictions significantly reduced working hours across workers of all ages. However, youth workers are more vulnerable than older workers to income and job loss in a crisis, because more young workers are hired via informal employment or non-standard forms of work, such as hourly or daily work, with high income and job uncertainty. They are more likely to experience outright job loss than temporary suspension. Given their shorter job tenure, businesses are less likely to retain them during lockdown periods (ILO and ADB 2020).

This situation is common across Asia and the Pacific, with nearly half of the youth working are employed in sectors that were hardest hit by the pandemic (ILO and ADB 2020). In Fiji, transport, other services,[4] and retail trade sectors account for 58.8% of total youth job loss. (Figure 1).

Figure 1: Distribution of Fiji's Youth Job Loss, by Sector, 2020

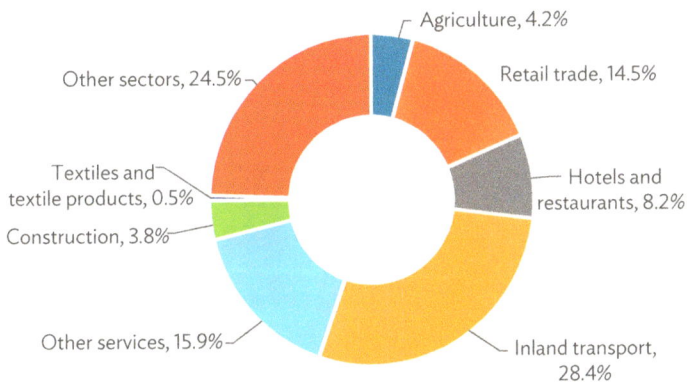

Notes:
1. Agriculture includes hunting, forestry, and fishing.
2. Retail excludes motor vehicles and motorcycles but includes repair of household goods.
3. Other services refer to other community, social, and personal services.
Source: International Labour Organization and Asian Development Bank. 2020. *Tackling the COVID-19 youth employment crisis in Asia and the Pacific.* Bangkok and Manila.

LABOR MIGRATION AND BRAIN DRAIN

Labor out-migration in Fiji has been steadily growing but remains moderate by South Pacific standards. A major driver has been Fiji's access to various labor mobility schemes that Australia and New Zealand have with Pacific developing member countries (DMCs).[5] Out of 34,400 Pacific workers employed in either Australia or New Zealand on one of the labor schemes, about 3,300 were from Fiji (Howes, Curtain, and Sharman 2022) (Figure 2).

More recently, migration for many Pacific DMCs has become more focused on skilled workers. In the case of Fiji, the pace of this emigration has left businesses in some sectors more susceptible to staff shortages. Anecdotes include a restaurant owner who lost four chefs and majority of her wait staff; and a coffee shop chain owner who lost 20 workers so far in 2022, with many leaving on short notice after securing their Australian visas (Burgess and Voloder 2022). This development has been particularly tricky, especially because the ramping up of overseas recruitment coincided with Fiji's reopening and start of economic recovery.

While concerns about brain drain may be dismissed if labor migration

is temporary, Curtain (2022a) argues that the short-term impact of worker scarcity can be more significant for small island countries. This is because a small-sized working population and pool of skilled workers limit opportunities to fill critical labor force gaps.

Figure 2: Workers from Pacific Developing Member Countries in Australia or New Zealand, Mid-2022

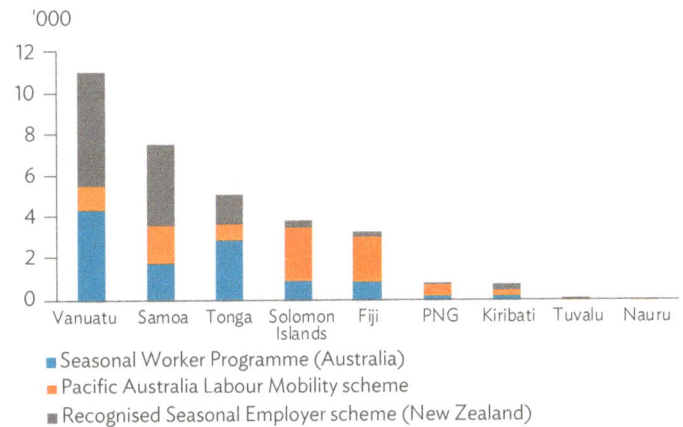

PNG = Papua New Guinea.
Source: S. Howes, R. Curtain, and E. Sharman. 2022. Labour mobility in the Pacific: transformational and/or negligible? *Devpolicy Blog.*

FACING THE HEADWINDS

These dual challenges of youth unemployment and skills gaps require both short- and long-term measures that should be designed to respond to the immediate needs as well as create sustainable programs that enhance the employability of young people. These targeted but large-scale strategies can contribute to the broader goals of poverty reduction, more inclusive labor markets for Fijians, and long-run sustainable growth.

The Government of Fiji has made significant advances in social protection, including the work toward the establishment of the *Social Assistance Policy: Protecting the Poor and Vulnerable* in 2021. According to the International Labour Organization, 58.9% of the population were covered by at least one social protection benefit in 2020. The government has proven its capacity to lead social protection support in response to emergencies and climatic disasters, such as during cyclones and COVID-19. This support has included providing income support to Fiji National Provident Fund members who did not have sufficient general account balances, increasing transfers to beneficiaries of social protection schemes, and providing income support to formal and informal workers who became unemployed because of COVID-19. Pre-COVID-19, social protection expenditures equaled 3.9% of GDP, providing benefits to about a third of Fiji's population. 24% of beneficiaries were enrolled in social insurance programs, 75% in social assistance programs, and 1% in active labor market programs in 2015 (ADB 2019). Yet more can always be done.

One short-term strategy that can be considered is a youth-targeted wage subsidy program. This would reduce the costs of recruitment, retention, and training, helping young people enter, reenter, or remain in the labor market. A joint study by the International Labour Organization and ADB recommended that, for the formal sector, this could take the form of lower employer contributions to the Fiji National Provident Fund (ILO and ADB 2020).

But given a prevalence of unemployed young workers, employment programs for the youth in the public sector would target the most vulnerable better. Immediate mobilization of subsidized placements can also help youth maintain attachment to productive activities. This is aligned with the government's strategy to reduce unemployment by increasing youth volunteerism and work attachment (Government of Fiji 2018). Those who meet the criteria are registered under Fiji's National Employment Centre. It was through this incentive that the government was able to easily mobilize Fiji's labor market supply to meet the demands in Australia and New Zealand since the pandemic.

Reducing job insecurity among young workers would require substantial investments in training, reskilling, and upskilling them. In the short term, training can strengthen labor market mobility and resilience. Training, including apprenticeship programs, can help match skills with ever-changing labor market needs, and thereby improve the chances of labor market reintegration (ILO and ADB 2020).

With formal education and training programs playing a crucial role in equipping young jobseekers with skills, the government must ensure that education and training policies and systems are aligned with labor market demand in growth sectors and occupations. One area that needs attention is the expansion of digital infrastructure and access, especially with the rise of online learning. Reliable connectivity, modern equipment, quality curricula, and competent digital skills for both students and educators are necessary to improve education and training and enhance education resilience in the event of disruptions.

Likewise, training is vital to address the problems that are arising from labor migration. Continuous training of workers should be an integral part of business strategy to ensure continuity of operations. Departing skilled workers who acquired skills through a combination of formal and on-the-job training poses a more serious problem as it creates "hard-to-fill skills gaps" (Curtain 2022b). While training remains the ultimate solution, Curtain argues that this responsibility goes beyond the businesses and should be done instead by both the source countries and recipient countries. In particular, he cites the role that the Australia Pacific Training Coalition plays in promoting labor mobility and combating brain drain. By having two tracks in its training program, it can provide training both for those who wish to seek overseas employment and those workers who will replace them.

The challenges posed by both rising youth unemployment and labor out-migration are significant as these can threaten the economy's strong recovery. To a certain extent, one can argue that these headwinds "complement" each other. Rising youth unemployment can be viewed as a growing untapped labor resource which can address the labor shortage needs of Fijian businesses who are severely affected by the massive out-migration of their former workers. This may be viewed as a simplistic approach to address concerns which are expected to have a long-term impact on the economy. Ultimately, quick solutions to these headwinds must be accompanied by responsive skilling programs and enabling policies that reduce the likelihood of labor shortages and migration issues. The government recognizes the concerns of Fijian businesses which are adversely affected by their workers' exodus from Fiji, but it understands also that availing such high-paying opportunities overseas is a right of the workers (Nair 2022; Devi 2022). Closer coordination and collaboration among stakeholders is necessary to address these issues.

Endnotes

[1] There were two unemployment rate figures that were estimated representing the short and long containment measures (ILO and ADB 2020).

[2] There was a break on employment and emigration detailed series in 2014 and 2015 which hinders comparison to before 2016.

[3] Only Fiji, Papua New Guinea, Samoa, Solomon Islands, Tonga, and Vanuatu have available data on youth unemployment rate figures in the World Bank database.

[4] Other services refer to other community, social, and personal services (ILO and ADB 2020).

[5] The three labor schemes that Australia and New Zealand currently have for Pacific developing member countries are the Seasonal Worker Programme of Australia, Recognised Seasonal Employer scheme of New Zealand, and the Pacific Australia Labour Mobility scheme (formerly the Pacific Labour Scheme).

References

Asian Development Bank (ADB). 2019. *The Social Protection Indicator for the Pacific*. Manila.

Burgess, A. and D. Voloder. 2022. Pacific Islands tourism sector struggling as staff leave under mobility scheme to meet Australia's worker shortage. *ABC News*.

Curtain, R. 2022a. Brain drain 1: a growing concern. *Devpolicy Blog*.

Curtain, R. 2022b. Brain drain 3: specific problems and solutions. *Devpolicy Blog*.

Devi, S. 2022. Labour scheme issue. *The Fiji Times*.

Government of Fiji, Bureau of Statistics. 2022. *2019–20 Household Income and Expenditure Survey Main Report*. Suva.

Government of Fiji, Bureau of Statistics; and International Labour Organization (ILO). 2018. *Fiji Employment and Unemployment Survey 2015–2016*. Suva.

Government of Fiji, Ministry of Employment, Productivity & Industrial Relations. 2018. *Strategic Development Plan 2018–2022*. Suva.

Howes, S., R. Curtain, and E. Sharman. 2022. Labour mobility in the Pacific: transformational and/or negligible? *Devpolicy Blog*.

ILO. ILOSTAT Database (accessed 23 November 2022).

ILO and ADB. 2020. *Tackling the COVID-19 youth employment crisis in Asia and the Pacific*. Bangkok and Manila.

International Organization for Migration. 2020. *Migration in the Republic of Fiji: A Country Profile 2020*. Geneva.

Nair, K. 2022. Skilled workers are not giving advanced notice when leaving for work in Australia – Bala. *FijiVillage*.

Wainiqolo, I. 2019. Labor productivity and youth unemployment in Fiji. *Pacific Economic Monitor*. ADB: Manila (December).

World Bank. World Bank Open Data (accessed 23 November 2022).

Social protection in the Federated States of Micronesia: Spotlight on subsistence and food security

Lead author: Remrick Patagan

The COVID-19 pandemic and the surge in inflation in many countries have renewed attention on social protection and food security[1] as invaluable planks of the development policy agenda. The pandemic exposed the inadequacy of current systems, and the rollout of emergency social assistance[2] became a key challenge to providing adequate social protection programs (Hondo et al. 2022). More than 2 years later, the easing of pandemic-related restrictions caused a rebound in consumption even as producers continue to grapple with supply chain disruptions and backlogs. The resulting inflation has been further amplified by the impacts of the Russian invasion of Ukraine, sharply increasing food and fuel prices with adverse effects on the most vulnerable sectors of society.

While prices of key international commodities, such as grains and edible oils, have declined from recent peaks, inflationary pressures have since broadened and costlier inputs cloud the outlook for food production. Understandably, food security has taken renewed urgency in many Pacific DMCs, given their dependence on imports and on subsistence agriculture and fishing activities. Because subsistence production also serves as an informal social safety net, it is integral to the goals of developing appropriate social protection systems and ensuring food security.

This article provides an overview of the state of social protection in the Federated States of Micronesia (FSM), and argues that policies supporting subsistence production are consistent with the pursuit of food security and long-term economic development. Where these policies help build resilience to economic and natural shocks, they can also become a worthwhile complement to the development of formal social protection measures not specifically related to agriculture and fisheries.

CURRENT STATE OF SOCIAL PROTECTION

The FSM had no formal social safety net programs prior to the COVID-19 pandemic, relying instead on traditional community obligations and norms regarding caring for vulnerable members of society. The government has yet to formulate an overarching social safety net policy, and there were no welfare programs for those outside the formal employment sector. Given the dominance of the public sector in the labor market, government employment is the closest equivalent to an institutionalized social protection system in that it provides livelihood, income, and other benefits to a large segment of the population.

Despite the outsized role of public employment, economic activity in the FSM still largely consists of subsistence farming and fishing. Widespread subsistence production serves as an informal social safety net for households faced with economic, and particularly food-related, shocks. More than 90% of those working in agricultural occupations are unpaid compared to an average of 60% for the entire labor force, indicating the extent of the informal economy and subsistence activity in agriculture. Production mainly for home consumption along with a long-run upward trend in the agricultural output suggests that households have historically turned to subsistence production to support themselves (Department of Resource and Development 2019).

Another alternative safety net is migration and the resulting flow of private remittances. This is especially important for households without cash employment opportunities although the extent of these flows is not adequately captured by official statistics. According to the Integrated Agriculture Census of 2016, the proportion of households reporting remittances as their main source of cash income increased to 19.5% in 2016 (from 13.0% in 2011), followed by pension at 8.8%. In Chuuk State, as many as 34.8% of households reported remittances as the biggest source of cash income relative to paid non-agricultural work at 26.2% and pension at 6.8%.

The abovementioned factors partly explain why formal safety nets and social protection measures have remained underdeveloped in the FSM. During the initial phase of the pandemic, however, the magnitude of social and economic disruption prompted

Table 4: Federated States of Micronesia Social Protection Program

Activity	Budget	Department	Particulars
Cash transfer	$6 million	Department of Finance and Administration	Cash transfer program to about 4,500 low-income households to provide temporary cash relief for households outside the formal labor sector, such as subsistence farmers and fishermen, and specifically laborers who do not qualify for the Pandemic Unemployment Assistance Program. Involves a one-time assistance of $1,000 to each household as encouragement to use this to enhance coronavirus disease (COVID-19) readiness, such as preventive items.
Food security	$2 million	Department of Resource and Development	Food security program for community groups and low-income households is intended to provide subsistence livelihood training, and an equitable distribution of seeds, planting, and fishing materials to vulnerable citizens at no cost.
Financial assistance to vulnerable groups	$1 million	Department of Health and Social Affairs	Intended beneficiaries are the elderly, persons with disabilities, and survivors of gender-based violence (GBV) to provide temporary waivers of medical expenses not included under funding from the Compact of Free Association; electricity subsidies to an estimated 2,000 low-income households with dependents with disabilities; distribution of solar lamps to an estimated 5,000 households on remote outer islands; and clinical management of rape and intimate partner violence kits and consultation options for survivors of GBV.
Community-based COVID-19	$2 million	Department of Health and Social Affairs	The community-based awareness grant is intended to strengthen COVID-19 awareness, including education on handwashing and social distancing; distribution of soaps, masks, and informational materials; and piloting a GBV hotline in Pohnpei State.

Source: Government of the Federated States of Micronesia, Department of Finance and Administration. Social Protection Program.

governments across the world to roll out social safety nets and stimulus measures. Development partners also included safety net and social protection provisions in their pandemic response and assistance packages.

Following the severe impact of the pandemic on the economy, the Government of the FSM launched a COVID-19 Response Framework to guide its mitigation efforts at the national and state levels. This was followed by a $58.7 million comprehensive countercyclical response program comprising a COVID-19 Health Action Plan for pandemic preparedness and response; an Economic Stimulus Package for affected businesses and workers; and a Social Protection Program for vulnerable groups (Table 4).

While the interventions implemented were intended to address immediate concerns and were not intended to be sustained beyond the crisis, they have laid the foundation for further development of the social protection system in the FSM. For instance, a low-income household survey led to a new database that could contribute to more sustainable and better-targeted programs in the future. More broadly, the government's comprehensive countercyclical response was aligned with the 2023 Action Plan that aims to enhance economic and fiscal sustainability focusing on improving public financial management. Sustainable financing is a prerequisite for institutionalized social protection programs (Hondo et al. 2022).

Apart from the temporary nature of the Social Protection Program, there were difficulties in implementation. Delayed and often incomplete reports posed a problem for monitoring and evaluation. This was attributed to capacity constraints in state governments, which are stretched thin by the pandemic response. Coordination issues between national and state governments also effectively stalled the community-driven food security component of the Social Protection Program. The importance of this component

cannot be overemphasized, given the significance of subsistence agriculture in the FSM, the integral role of communities in informal social safety nets, and the close linkage between food security and the broader social protection agenda.

IMPORTANCE OF AGRICULTURE AND FISHERIES

The agriculture sector and domestic fishing continue to provide food and livelihood to a significant proportion of the population in the FSM. Subsistence activities based on localized, small-scale production in family farms accounted for an estimated 16%–18% of GDP in 2005–2007, while commercial agriculture remains underdeveloped. Nevertheless, the contribution of subsistence agriculture is likely underestimated. The informal sector plays an important and often unacknowledged role in the economy. Seventy-seven percent of the population live in rural areas and are engaged in either pure or mixed subsistence production for their livelihoods. Food grown in family farms and home gardens is primarily for home consumption (FSM Agricultural Policy 2012–2016).

The government considers agriculture as a key priority for long-term economic development. Its Agriculture Policy states that the sector is crucial for livelihood and food security, espousing a culturally sensitive, community-based approach. Agriculture is central to ensuring health,[3] providing social safety nets, and preserving traditional culture. Food production on family farms and subsistence fishing continue to be a vital part of food security and a risk-coping strategy that provides resilience to economic shocks and disasters.

SUBSISTENCE AS SAFETY NET

Household vulnerability to poverty and hunger is most often associated with threats to livelihoods and can increase over time with repeated shocks that erode productive assets. This can be addressed by appropriate social protection measures that are most effective when delivering social assistance, while simultaneously preserving or building productive assets that reduce the risk of future insecurity. Such an approach requires strong linkages between social protection and complementary sectors, such as agriculture, health, and education (HLPE-FSN 2012).

In the FSM, subsistence production serves as a social safety net because of its largely agricultural economy. Policies that complement informal arrangements for managing risks, including traditional subsistence practices, therefore, could serve as an indirect social safety net that complements a broader social protection system. The country's small economy, geographical remoteness, and exposure to climate risks that make it vulnerable to economic shocks mean that developing formal social protection instruments is relatively more costly than in other DMCs. Thus, it makes more sense to focus on social assistance that enhances the incomes of farmers and fisherfolk and works through existing traditional practices. This is consistent also with best practice on the design of safety net programs that recommend the use of public resources to reinforce private systems (World Bank 2008).

This is not to say that formal social protection instruments should be eschewed in favor of informal social safety nets. It bears noting that advocating subsistence production is a second-best option that considers existing constraints and the country-specific context (de Janvry and Sadoulet 2011). Nevertheless, there are compelling arguments for supporting subsistence activities.

For one, it raises farm output and incomes, contributing to food security and economic development, which is consistent with public priorities. Greater agricultural production promotes food security by enhancing availability and access to food. It also complements efforts to improve dietary sources with better nutrition and health outcomes supporting poverty reduction and resilience. Given limited commercial agriculture, strengthening subsistence production can serve as a stepping stone for greater market participation, supporting the transition to commercial agriculture, and further agricultural development. Surplus production can be diverted to trading and selling, which can enhance incomes and reduce poverty and economic vulnerability.

In the context of high and volatile international food prices, de Janvry and Sadoulet (2011) argue that food security cannot be achieved without a productive subsistence production sector. Given market failures, weak administrative capacities, and large fiscal burdens in the FSM, subsistence farming can become a more economical means of promoting food security for vulnerable people. Crisis response via subsistence production makes economic sense because farmers tend to have low productivity, and ready access to land and extra labor (FAO 2006).

Further, well-designed social protection instruments should be context-specific, complementing existing coping strategies and building on local mechanisms for resilience (Cromwell and Slater 2004). Subsistence production is one such coping strategy in the FSM and is a cost-effective means for enhancing an informal social safety net while facilitating market access and income diversification.

Supporting subsistence production includes further improvements in agricultural policy that integrates food security and climate change considerations, along with greater use of vulnerability assessments and evidence-based decision-making. Another area of support would be public investments in agriculture and fisheries through infrastructure (transport and storage) and support services (provision of technical and managerial know-how, inputs, equipment, and shared facilities). Execution remains a challenge, however, with insufficient public resources and institutional capacity being major constraints. Continued support from development partners for relevant authorities at the national and state levels is necessary while learning from previous efforts should be pursued continuously. A deeper look into the challenges faced by the food security component of the Social Protection Program might be a good place to start.

The government can build on the successful components of the Social Protection Program toward the development of an institutionalized social protection system. Measures relating to subsistence production that can be implemented in the short term could focus on expanding and improving the provision of agricultural inputs and extension services. Beneficiaries can reduce costs by providing land and labor, while a community-driven approach can also help lighten the administrative burden. In the long term, the government must continue to pursue fiscal sustainability to facilitate public investments in agricultural infrastructure and research and development. Insurance for crops and natural resource assets could also complement social safety nets, but these would depend on data availability, along with creating an enabling market environment that is conducive to the development of such products.

Endnotes

[1]   Food security exists when all people, at all times, have physical and economic access to sufficient, safe, and nutritious food to meet their dietary needs and food preferences for an active and healthy life (World Food Summit 1996).

[2]   For purposes of this discussion, social assistance and safety nets are used interchangeably. Social assistance provides protection to those who cannot qualify for social insurance or, otherwise, would receive inadequate benefits.

[3]   Local foods are primarily composed of traditional crops along with fresh seafood. These have generally superior nutritional and health qualities compared to imported foods, which are mostly convenience starch foods, such as rice and flour-based products.

References

Cromwell, E. and R. Slater. 2004. *Food security and social protection.* September.

de Janvry, A. and E. Sadoulet. 2011. Subsistence farming as a safety net for food-price shock. *Development in Practice,* Volume 21, Numbers 4–5. June.

Englberger, L. and E. Johnson. 2013. *Traditional foods of the Pacific: Go Local, a case study in Pohnpei, Federated States of Micronesia.*

Food and Agriculture Organization of the United Nations (FAO). 2006. Food Security. *Policy Brief,* Issue 2. June.

Government of the FSM. 2014. *Household Income and Expenditure Survey 2013/2014: Main Analysis Report.* Palikhir, Pohnpei (December).

Government of the FSM, Department of Resource and Development. 2019. *Integrated Agriculture Census 2016.* Palikhir, Pohnpei.

Government of the FSM, Information Services. 2020. *The FSM COVID-19 Response Framework: A Summary.* Press Release. April.

Government of the FSM, Department of Finance and Administration. 2020. *FSM Social Protection Program.* Palikhir, Pohnpei.

Government of the FSM, Department of Finance and Administration. 2015. *FSM 2023 Action Plan.* Palikhir, Pohnpei.

Government of the FSM, Department of Resource and Development. *2012–2016 FSM Agricultural Policy.* Palikhir, Pohnpei.

High Level Panel of Experts on Food Security and Nutrition (HLPE-FSN). 2012. *Social Protection for food security: A report by the High Level Panel of Experts on Food Security and Nutrition of the Committee on World Food Security.* Rome (June).

Hondo, D., J. Haberl, and L. Arthur. 2022. *Redesigning social protection programs beyond the COVID-19 pandemic.* Asia Pathways: Asian Development Bank Institute Blog. Tokyo (4 November).

United Nations Educational, Scientific and Cultural Organization (UNESCO) Institute of Statistics. *Federated States of Micronesia Country Profile* (accessed 23 November 2022).

World Bank. 2008. *For protection and promotion: The design and implementation of effective safety nets.*

World Food Summit. 1996. *Rome Declaration on World Food Security.* Rome (November).

Forging sustainable social protection programs in Kiribati and Tuvalu

Lead authors: Lily-Anne Homasi, Isoa Wainiqolo, and Noel Del Castillo

When the pandemic forced countries to close their borders, Pacific DMCs mobilized COVID-19 response packages to support their economies and assist their citizens. Social protection was a vital component of these packages, with an average of almost 30% being for aid to the most vulnerable groups, but this varied significantly across countries (Carandang and Del Castillo 2020).

As countries reopen their economies to the world, pandemic-specific social protection schemes are expected to taper off. Even the broader social protection programs may need to be reevaluated for other national priority spending programs. This is particularly relevant for smaller economies, such as Kiribati and Tuvalu, where narrow economic bases limit the ability of governments to generate additional revenue to support higher spending. This article looks at specific social protection programs of Kiribati and Tuvalu and recommends guidelines for improving the sustainability of these programs, including upskilling and creating job opportunities to promote poverty reduction and resilience of vulnerable groups.

In many parts of the world, including the Pacific, social protection is an important component of government spending to promote and support the welfare of vulnerable groups—women, children, elderly, and persons with disabilities. Such support is considered a human right that is enshrined in many international treaties and commitments such as the Sustainable Development Goals. Social protection programs vary, with some well-established as in the case of the Cook Islands (supported by New Zealand) and some still underdeveloped, mainly in small island nations where the capacity to institutionalize is limited. In certain areas, governments might consider expanding available programs while ensuring their sustainability and effectiveness in reducing poverty and promoting resilience of vulnerable groups amid fiscal constraints.

KIRIBATI

In Kiribati, social protection programs are governed by various legislations including the 2013 Children, Young People and Family Welfare Act. Poverty is a key driver for such programs. According to the Government of Kiribati (2022), in 2019, 21.9% of the population were living in poverty.[1] Majority of the poor live in South Tarawa, the capital of Kiribati. Prior to the pandemic, spending on social protection was equivalent to about 8% of GDP. However, with elevated poverty levels during the pandemic, this tripled to 24% of GDP (Government of Kiribati 2022).

Expenditure on social protection accounted for 10% of the Government of Kiribati's National COVID-19 Preparedness and Response Plan. In 2021, almost 58% of the allocation for social protection went to the unemployment benefit program, as border closures resulted in job losses and more than 50,000 people benefited from the unemployment support (Government of Kiribati). This is illustrated in Figure 3, which shows that the share of social protection in the total recurrent expenditure significantly increased from a pre-pandemic average of about 13% to an average of 26% for the period 2020–2022.

Figure 3: Kiribati Spending on Social Protection

% of total recurrent expenditure

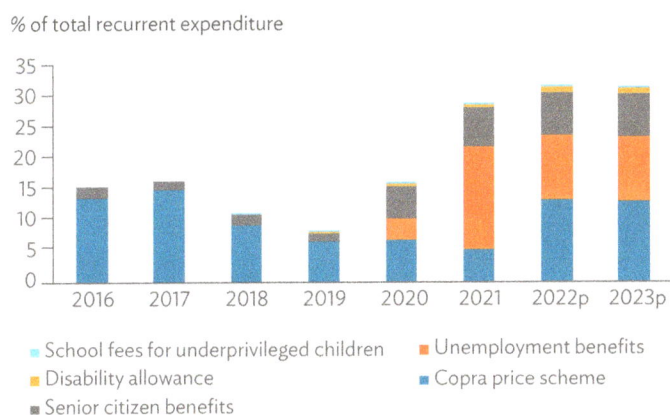

- School fees for underprivileged children
- Unemployment benefits
- Disability allowance
- Copra price scheme
- Senior citizen benefits

p = projection.
Source: ADB calculations using data from Government of Kiribati. *Recurrent Budget*. Tarawa (7 years: 2016–2022).

The Copra Price Subsidy, Senior Citizens Benefit, School Fee Support for Underprivileged Children, Disability Support Allowance, and, more recently, Unemployment Benefit comprise the formal social protection programs of Kiribati. Although the Kiribati Provident Fund has potential social protection aims, the main cash transfer programs are the Copra Price Subsidy and the Senior Citizens Benefit.

The Copra Price Subsidy is the largest formal social protection program of Kiribati. While the primary objective of the program is to maintain copra production, which is a main export, there are other secondary objectives (Kidd and Mackenzie 2012; Webb 2020). Given the growing problems concerning urbanization, the subsidy encourages people to remain on the outer islands rather than migrate to South Tarawa, Kiribati's capital, by providing income to the islands and sustaining island economies. Although it has followed a declining trend since 2017, the budget allocated for the Copra Price Subsidy jumped 150% in 2022 as the government budgeted A$40 million and is intending to maintain the same level next year (Government of Kiribati 2021).

Next in line is the unemployment payment, which the government introduced in 2020. From an initial allocation of A$8.6 million, it soared 485% in 2021 as the government accounted for the impact of the pandemic-induced border closures on the livelihood of many I-Kiribatis. Its share in the total recurrent expenditure expanded from a mere 4.1% in 2020 to 18.0% in 2021. In the same year, Kiribati recorded its first fiscal deficit since 2012 equal to 23.4% of GDP. While the government has budgeted a lower allocation for unemployment

benefit in 2022, it is still expected to grab a substantial share in the country's operating expenditure in the next 2 years.

Despite having a steady level of growth in its revenue streams and cash buffers, sustaining these types of social protection programs can become a challenge on the back of volatile revenue streams, such as fishing license fees. Also, continuing to maintain the same levels of financing for these programs, particularly the unemployment benefit and copra subsidy, reduces the resources available for transformational investments, such as education and training, which will upgrade the development prospects of Kiribati.

Training and upskilling are crucial factors to improve the employability of I-Kiribati workers. The government, through the Kiribati Institute of Technology, can consider a collaboration with development partners to introduce internship programs on the large infrastructure projects that are being undertaken in the country. Allowing students and trainees of the Kiribati Institute of Technology to do on-the-job training in such project sites will provide them with valuable training and skills that can increase their employability domestically and internationally. These upskilling initiatives could also increase the number of entrepreneurs that are servicing the domestic sector, and improve the share of the private sector in supporting Kiribati's development aspirations.

Rationalizing and improving the sustainability of its primary social programs can help the government to dedicate more of its resources to invest in education, health, and infrastructure development. With the support of development partners, investments in these important drivers of human development can help its people reduce dependency on social welfare benefits.

TUVALU

Tuvalu's formal social protection is concentrated on the Senior Citizen Scheme, accounting for 88% of government spending on social protection. The effective coverage for older persons is 19.5%, while 3.0% of the population received payments under the Senior Citizens Scheme.[2] Another component of the social insurance program is coursed through the Tuvalu National Provident Fund, which collects compulsory contributions from all employees, but excludes those operating in the informal economy. Like in most Pacific countries, Tuvalu primarily relies on traditional safety nets based on family and community linkages. These informal mechanisms have been effective in dealing with idiosyncratic shocks but are vulnerable to emigration and depopulation of outer islands as well as large common shocks, such as the COVID-19 pandemic.

In 2018, the government reviewed its financial support scheme for people who are living with disabilities, which is part of the Tuvalu Social Development Policy 2016, and put in place the Tuvalu National Policy for Disability. In 2019, the government increased monthly payments under the Senior Citizen Scheme (70 years old and above) from A$70 per person to A$100.

Household Income and Expenditure Surveys are conducted regularly to identify the poor based on location, ethnicity, gender, age, level of education, main sources of income and household characteristics. The

2015–2016 survey identified vulnerable groups such as the elderly, children, and women. However, with government spending focused on outer islands, for provision of education and health facilities, electricity subsidies, inter-island transport and emergency services, information and communication technology infrastructure, and a price equalization program (import freight levy),[3] less resources are available to assist the vulnerable groups of the population.

Education is free and compulsory for children ages 6–15. Expenditure on education increased from 13% of total government expenditure in 2012 to more than 18% in 2019, immediately before the pandemic.

Tuvalu's COVID-19 response package allocated 56% of its funding to social protection spending. Without a formal social protection mechanism, the government focused on direct cash payout of A$80 to all Tuvaluans and an additional A$80 for households with total income below A$80 per month. The government has likewise allowed members of the Tuvalu National Provident Fund to withdraw up to A$500 per month from their savings accounts for 3 months as well as flexibility on repayments of existing loans.

Tuvalu's social protection budget (which includes grants, subsidies, and donations; the medical treatment scheme; and scholarship/training) made up an average of 15.8% of total expenditures in 2018 and 2019 which increased to 24.1% since the pandemic (Figure 4). Grants, subsidies, and donations ranged between 5% and 7% of total expenditure between 2018 and 2020, while the medical scheme averaged 6% of expenditures. The bulk of scholarships is taken up by tertiary education.

Figure 4: Tuvalu Spending on Social Protection

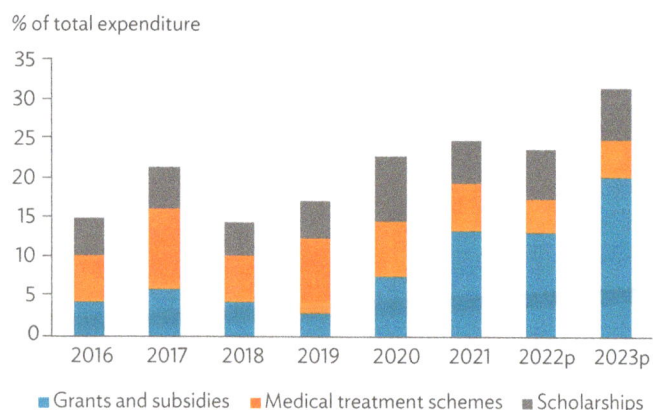

% of total expenditure

■ Grants and subsidies　■ Medical treatment schemes　■ Scholarships

p = projection.
Source: ADB calculations using data from Government of Tuvalu. *National Budget*. Funafuti (7 years: 2016–2022).

The Government of Tuvalu is making efforts to improve education and health. The Ministry of Education, Youth, and Sports and the Ministry of Health, Social Welfare, and Gender Affairs were both allocated 12.8% of total expenditures in the 2022 budget. Lower secondary completion rate as a percentage of relevant age group

fell to below 65% in 2019 and 2020 compared to a high 96% in 2014. However, its education scholarship program may need to be refocused to primary and secondary levels because of low enrollment rates compared to similar countries. Also, it may need to introduce technical and vocational education and training programs for the benefit of those with some form of education.

While the medical scheme is mostly used by the elderly, the introduction in 2021 of taxes on products that are considered unhealthy can hopefully reduce the number of individuals availing of medical facilities.

Raising voluntary contribution to the Tuvalu National Provident Fund may also bode well in the future, provided that proper withdrawal constraints are put in place. Ensuring that there are sufficient funds set aside for retirement may reduce the need for the Senior Citizens Scheme over time.

LOOKING AHEAD

Social protection is an integral component of the commitment of the governments of Kiribati and Tuvalu to provide social safety nets to their citizens. However, the sustainability of social protection programs is under threat, given fiscal constraints and development challenges that are impacting growth prospects for these island nations. Some of the key measures to sustain such programs are discussed below.

Design targeted social protection programs. Properly targeting the beneficiaries of these programs can avoid leakages and wasted resources and ensure that the programs are cost-effective. These should be developed drawing on multidimensional social assessments to determine the living status of the population. Assessments on current support to vulnerable groups would help inform the challenges and issues that the government would need to address through tailored technical and financial support. Involving a multi-sectoral solutions team should help to ensure that the social protection program is targeted, has the buy-in of stakeholders, and provides clarity on the management of such critical support.

Strengthen the governance and management arrangements. There should be guidelines articulating the governance and management arrangements and the roles of parties involved. Existing programs could be reviewed with a view to incorporate lessons from managing the current social protection programs. In the case of a governing body (steering committee) overseeing social protection matters in these countries, there is a need to involve key stakeholders, including the ministries of finance, education, health, social welfare, and local government, and gender and climate change departments. The operational guidelines for each type of social protection program should be clearly articulated in terms of steps to administer it and steps for the public to access it, with this information made available publicly.

Review and update social protection legal framework and practice. Some of the legislation guiding social protection programs is outdated; governments may need to update and strengthen it. This could involve reviewing current legislation, existing social protection programs, and the fiscal implications of these programs. Governments need to ensure that revisions to the legal framework have considered the sustainability of the programs. This should improve alignment between the legal framework and practice.

Establish partnerships (internally and externally) – technical knowledge and financing. Governments generally have limited technical and financial resources to sustain social protection programs. Hence, establishing and deepening partnerships to refine these schemes is critical.

- **Internally.** Leverage support to review and restructure existing programs for efficiencies.
- **Externally.** Secure technical expertise and financing to support tailored and targeted social protection programs, e.g., labor mobility schemes. This could also include capacity-building initiatives to support Kiribati and Tuvalu in administering their social protection programs in an efficient and effective manner.

Endnotes

[1] The poverty line is constructed using the 2019/20 Household Income and Expenditure Survey and is based on an annual per adult equivalent consumption of A$1,705 (or equivalent to $4.32 2011 per day on a purchasing power parity basis) (Government of Kiribati 2022).

[2] Effective coverage for older age is defined as a share of population above statutory pensionable age receiving old-age pension.

[3] This is a program that ensures that goods sold in the outer islands are charged the same prices as in Funafuti, the capital of Tuvalu.

References

Carandang, N. and N. Del Castillo. 2020. Social protection and COVID-19 in the Pacific: economic inoculation to mitigate the impacts of the pandemic. *Pacific Economic Monitor*. Manila: ADB (December).

Government of Kiribati. 2013. *Children, Young People and Family Welfare Act*. Tarawa.

Government of Kiribati, Ministry of Women, Youth, Sports, and Social Affairs.

Government of Kiribati, National Statistics Office. 2022. *Poverty in Kiribati: Based on Analysis of the 2019/20 Household Income and Expenditure Survey*. Nouméa: Pacific Community.

Government of Kiribati. *Recurrent Budget*. Tarawa (7 years: 2016–2022).

Government of Tuvalu. *National Budget*. Funafuti (7 years: 2016–2022).

Kidd, S. and U. Mackenzie. 2012. *Kiribati country case study – AusAID Pacific Social Protection Series: Poverty, Vulnerability and Social Protection in the Pacific*. Canberra: Australian Agency for International Development.

United Nations. Sustainable Development Goals.

Webb, J. 2020. Kiribati economic survey: Oceans of opportunity. *Asia & the Pacific Policy Studies*. 7(1). pp. 5–26.

Pondering post-pandemic social protection in the Marshall Islands

Lead author: Cara Tinio

THE BENEFITS OF SWIFT AND DECISIVE ACTION

Recognizing the significant socioeconomic risks presented by the COVID-19 pandemic, and its limited capacity to mitigate these risks and their impacts, the Government of the Marshall Islands promptly imposed border restrictions when the virus began to emerge in January 2020. Although this prevented community transmission of COVID-19 until August 2022—giving the government time to strengthen its health systems and protocols, as well as vaccinate the population—the extended period of restrictions hampered the flow of goods into the heavily import-dependent country, dampened business activity, and stalled the implementation of public infrastructure projects. The resulting economic slowdown has reduced employment and incomes, spelling increased hardship especially for vulnerable communities and households, as well as reduced government revenues. The fallout of the pandemic has also increased the possibility of worsening gender inequalities and undoing progress made in women's economic empowerment.

The government's Coronavirus Preparedness and Response Plan, approved in June 2020 and implemented in FY2020 (ended 30 September 2020) and FY2021, included a substantial social protection component that, among others, supported households in the more remote parts of the Marshall Islands and expanded water, sanitation, and hygiene facilities as well as the Ministry of Education's school feeding program. Another component supported continuity and recovery for businesses adversely affected by the travel restrictions. The plan also outlined measures to strengthen the health system's capacity for surveillance, infection control, and case management; keep essential services running; and provide consular assistance to citizens abroad. Alongside the plan, the government continued to implement pre-pandemic social protection programs targeting vulnerable groups.

ADB supported the implementation of the plan through a comprehensive package of support that included the Health Expenditure and Livelihoods Support (HEALS) Program under the COVID-19 Pandemic Response Option (CPRO) modality. The program grant of $16.0 million, equivalent to 35% of the cost required to implement the plan, funded social assistance programs, financial relief for businesses and workers, countercyclical government spending, and continuation of essential services and employment. Besides the CPRO modality, ADB provided contingent disaster financing to support immediate response measures; helped procure COVID-19 test kits, personal protective equipment, and medical supplies; and supported community outreach about the disease. Other ADB resources funded a rapid assessment of the social impacts on vulnerable groups of the COVID-19-related pause in economic activity; and supported the government in assessing the pandemic's effects on external resource inflows and small and medium-sized enterprises, refining its macro-fiscal framework and responses to external shocks, and strengthening capacity to implement fiscal sustainability reforms.

The HEALS Program helped the government to achieve at least substantially many of the social protection and economic relief targets set under the plan, enabling the following:

- Provision to all 2,380 targeted households of food baskets containing supplies sufficient for an extended period (to reduce logistical burden of monthly deliveries). The government is monitoring the need for follow-on deliveries.
- Delivery of fishing gear and farming tools to at least 73% of 19 of the 23 target islands and atolls. (Logistical challenges precluded the full achievement of this target.)
- Expansion of the Ministry of Education's school feeding program from the existing 3 days a week to 5 days a week, and provision of one meal a day to 10,272 school children (49% of whom were girls) from government-identified low-income families during the 2020–2021 academic year.
- Distribution of 647 water, sanitation, and hygiene and dignity kits to women and girls from vulnerable households in Majuro. The plan targeted distribution of 700 kits in Majuro and Ebeye, but the delivery to Ebeye was deferred because the KAN Group in Kwajalein had already distributed similar kits in the area.
- Establishment of two gender-based violence (GBV) telephone hotlines in Majuro, with advisory support from a local nongovernment organization, and one hotline with similar support in Ebeye.
- Extension of economic relief assistance to 416 business owners, 155 of whom were women and including small and medium-sized enterprise owners, whose operations were adversely affected by COVID-19 travel restrictions. Three hundred Majuro taxi drivers also received support.
- Retention of all national government employees. The number of national public servants even rose from 2,488 at the end of FY2019 to 2,599 (31% of whom are women) at the end of FY2021.

These measures were instrumental in avoiding cases of food poverty or hunger while borders were closed. The expanded school feeding program had the additional benefits of reducing disruptions to education by maintaining consistent school attendance. Meanwhile, the dignity kits helped ensure that women and girls continued to observe safe hygiene practices.

Economic relief provided under the plan staved off a larger reduction in household incomes and helped to avert a projected 9.3%–12.4%

increase in the poverty rate than would have been realized under a scenario without mitigation programs and unemployment benefits. Assistance to entrepreneurs allowed them to retain workers and, as a result, 222 full-time jobs were estimated to have been lost in FY2021 compared with the 417–716 projected at the start of the HEALS Program; while support to informal workers, most of whom did not have savings or access to social safety nets, saw them through the period of diminished business activity. Further, ensuring that government workers kept their jobs ensured steady provision of public services. The HEALS Program also helped meet the plan's health system targets by safeguarding public well-being and preventing community transmission of COVID-19 until August 2022.

ADB's future assistance to the Marshall Islands is expected to lean toward facilitating recovery from the COVID-19 crisis. This involves continuing investments in strengthened health care systems as well as in essential infrastructure, including energy and water and sanitation, and building and supplementing government implementation capacity. Other innovative interventions will be explored, such as supporting youth, particularly young women, to access employment and productive livelihoods.

SUSTAINING SOCIAL PROTECTION AMID GROWING CONCERNS

Substantial grant inflows in recent years, including ADB assistance under the CPRO modality, led to fiscal expansion largely because of additional pandemic response spending and helped the government realize fiscal surpluses in FY2020–FY2021 (Figure 5). The International Monetary Fund (IMF) recommends that assistance should continue until the economy is firmly on its way to recovery, with further refinements to prioritization and targeting. However, the Marshall Islands faces a formidable challenge as development partner grants to support COVID-19 response wind down and grants from the US expire. Fiscal deficits are seen in future years.

Figure 5: Government Expenditures and Fiscal Balances in the Marshall Islands

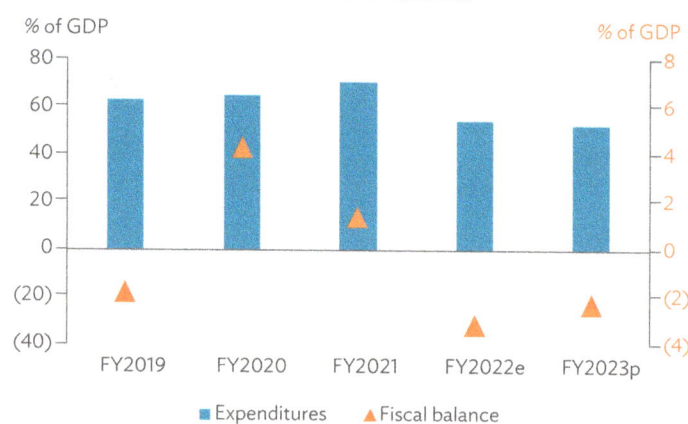

e = estimate, FY = fiscal year, GDP = gross domestic product, p = projection.
Note: Fiscal year ends 30 September of that year.
Sources: ADB. 2022. *Completion Report: Health Expenditure and Livelihoods Support Program in the Marshall Islands.* Manila; and Asian Development Outlook database (accessed 2 November 2022).

Boosted by development partner grants, expenditure reached unsustainable levels during the pandemic and now requires downward adjustments to fit the still-recovering resource envelope. At the same time, grants under the country's Compact of Free Association with the US as well as a supplemental education grant (SEG) are scheduled to end in FY2023, exerting further pressure to reduce expenditures. These grants are channeled mostly toward education and health and, in FY2019, covered about 25% and 49% of health and education spending, respectively. The Compact also supports provision by the US of a range of postal, weather, aviation, and disaster assistance services that are scheduled to end in 2023–2024.

The US Government Accountability Office (2022) expects that the end of the Compact grants, SEG, and some services in 2023 will bring about fiscal gaps for the government. Although the government established a Compact Trust Fund, this may not realize enough returns to offset expired Compact grants, especially over the longer term, or provide disbursements every year (Figure 6). Further, there are no provisions to offset the SEG or self-fund the services scheduled to end in 2023–2024.

Figure 6: Marshall Islands Compact Trust Fund Outlook

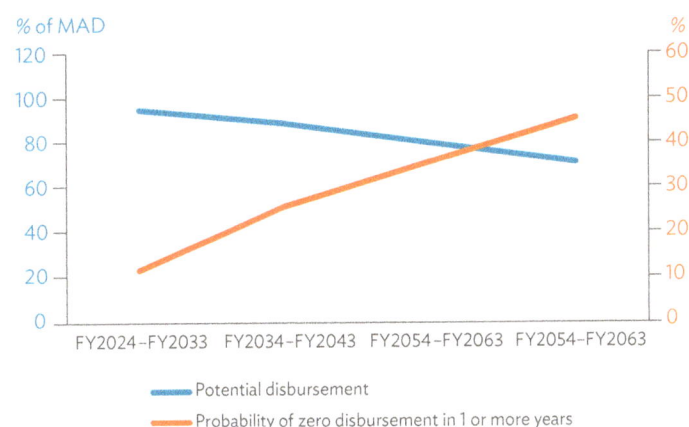

FY = fiscal year, MAD = maximum allowable disbursement.

Notes:

1. Fiscal year ends 30 September of that year.

2. Maximum allowable disbursement is equal to the FY2023 Compact grants ($26.7 million), adjusted for inflation.

Source: United States Government Accountability Office. 2022. *Compacts of Free Association: Implications of Planned Ending of Some U.S. Economic Assistance*. Washington, DC.

Although renewal of the Compact is under discussion, the Marshall Islands still faces the possibility that financing needs, especially for education, health, and social protection, will be sizable after FY2023. This places the country at high risk of debt distress according to the IMF (2021) despite public debt levels remaining sustainable. Together with continued implementation of reforms, development partner grants will be crucial in helping to manage the risk of debt distress as well as strengthening the country's fiscal and structural foundations.

CONCLUSION AND RECOMMENDATIONS

The Marshall Islands' quick implementation of border containment measures delayed the domestic outbreak of COVID-19 until August 2022, and the government's response plan helped mitigate the pandemic's socioeconomic impacts on the population. Continuing support, especially to the most vulnerable, is needed while the economy recovers; and the implementation of ADB's HEALS Program highlights some factors to consider in crafting social protection policies for the Marshall Islands and similar economies in the Pacific.

- **Context-driven design, implementation, and monitoring.** ADB aligned the HEALS Program with the government's pandemic response plan, designing assistance measures based on findings from a rapid vulnerability and needs assessment. Activities targeting the health and safety of women and girls, and prioritizing their inclusion in socioeconomic assistance measures, helped safeguard their well-being as the economy adjusted to closed borders.

  The HEALS Program gave due consideration to implementation capacity constraints on the ground; arising from the Marshall Islands being a fragile, small island developing state, these constraints were exacerbated by the pandemic. Conscious efforts to use existing reporting mechanisms helped avoid additional administrative burdens on the government, whose capacity was already stretched thin by the pandemic response. Harmonizing reporting requirements across development partners would help to reduce these burdens further.

- **Collaboration, coordination, and complementarity.** ADB developed the HEALS Program in close collaboration with the government and development partners. For instance, the International Organization for Migration conducted the rapid assessment that informed program design, while coordination with the IMF helped ensure that the program would safeguard macroeconomic stability.

  Close coordination with the government was also instrumental. Keeping the government's detailed response plan at the heart of development partner efforts avoided duplications. Regular meetings—enabled by ADB's strong in-country presence through its Pacific Country Office as well as an ongoing public financial management project—facilitated communications, coordination, and monitoring, supporting program implementation and heading off any emerging implementation-related issues. Advisory services via the Ministry of Finance's Reform Coordination Unit, established through the ongoing ADB project to strengthen local capacity to implement reforms, helped the ministry to design, deliver, and monitor COVID-19 assistance measures effectively. This was instrumental in meeting plan targets.

However, resources for social protection initiatives will be tight, given the winding down of COVID-19 grants from development partners and looming expiration of assistance from the US. It is imperative for the Marshall Islands to ensure that social protection initiatives are funded alongside other essential public services and investments. To this end, ADB will continue to support the crafting and implementation of public sector reforms in tax policy and administration, nontax revenue management, contingent liabilities, performance-based budgeting, and state-owned enterprise efficiency. Other areas requiring government attention include domestic resource mobilization and expenditure rationalization.

References

Asian Development Bank (ADB). 2020. *Marshall Islands: Health Expenditure and Livelihoods Support Program.* Manila.

Graduate School USA. 2022. *2022 Economic Brief: Republic of the Marshall Islands.*

International Monetary Fund. 2021. *Republic of the Marshall Islands: 2021 Article IV Consultation—Press Release; Staff Report; and Statement by the Executive Director for the Republic of the Marshall Islands.* Washington, DC.

Tinio, C. and R. Rabanal. 2020. Addressing the economic challenges of COVID-19 in the Federated States of Micronesia and the Marshall Islands. *Pacific Economic Monitor.* Manila: ADB (December).

United States Government Accountability Office. 2022. *Compacts of Free Association: Implications of Planned Ending of Some U.S. Economic Assistance.*

Gearing up: Nauru's new social protection strategy

Lead authors: Jacqueline Connell and Prince Cruz

Nauru's social protection is dominated by social assistance programs, while labor market and social insurance programs are still underdeveloped. In May 2022, the Government of Nauru launched the National Social Protection Strategy 2022–2032 to reform the system.[1] Promoting labor market programs to help address Nauru's high youth unemployment is a key aspect of the strategy, as well as ensuring the financial sustainability of social protection. This will be challenging. Even before programs are upgraded, the costs of the aged pension will approximately double over the next 2 decades. Careful expenditure prioritization and mobilization of domestic resources will likely be needed to ensure social protection for future generations.

Nauru has a long history of government provision of social benefits and free health and education services to its citizens. Social assistance programs include birth and death claims, disability allowances, aged pension, and education support programs. The coverage of programs is relatively wide. For instance, 84.6% of people with a severe disability received a disability social protection benefit in 2020, compared to Fiji (20.1%) and Tonga (20.2%) (SPC 2021).

To encourage students to remain in school, the Nauru Education Assistance Trust (NEAT) scheme was introduced in 2016. It provides a A$5 per day conditional cash transfer to school-aged students for school attendance. This amounts to about A$1,000 for each school year. The entitlement is accrued and paid on completion of grade 12. If a child fails to complete grade 9, they will forfeit the accrued entitlements (Government of Nauru 2016). The government has also provided free school lunches to all students since 2014.[2]

In addition to the government-funded aged pension, Nauru has a defined-contribution superannuation scheme to support people in retirement.[3] Employers and employees each contribute 5% of the superannuable salary. The benefit can be withdrawn upon retirement from aged 55. Following its expansion in 2019, the Nauru Superannuation Scheme covers formal sector employees aged 18 and above. There were 4,528 employee members of the Nauru Superannuation Scheme in June 2021 (Government of Nauru 2021). This relatively wide coverage of about 65% of eligible population partly reflects Nauru's small subsistence sector, which is not covered by the scheme.[4]

During the COVID-19 pandemic, government spending on social protection climbed from 3.1% of GDP in FY2019 (ended 30 June 2019) to 5.6% in FY2021–FY2022 (Figure 7).[5] The government increased the payment rates of the aged and disability pensions, and raised spending on the school feeding program. Quarterly "back-to-school" cash payments were introduced to help parents purchase school items, such as uniforms and shoes. Ex-gratia stimulus payments were also paid to government employees, including state-owned enterprises workers, and Nauruans receiving a pension or living with a disability to offset rising living costs. The government maintained these measures in the FY2023 budget with total allocation rising to 6.3% of GDP.

Figure 7: Nauru Social Protection Spending

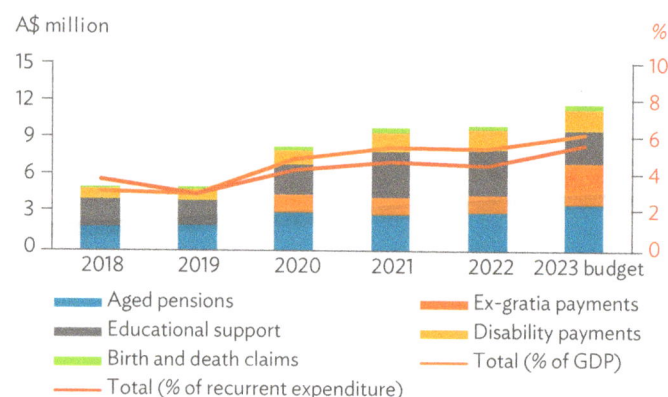

GDP = gross domestic product.

Notes:

1. Years are fiscal years ending on 30 June of that year.

2. Educational support includes back-to-school, Nauru Educational Assistance Trust (NEAT) Scheme, and the school lunch program.

Sources: ADB estimates; and Government of Nauru. GON budgets. Yaren (5 years: 2018–2022).

Although social protection in Nauru is more extensive compared to most other Pacific countries, there are gaps in the provision of safety nets for working-age adults, including informal workers. Also, there are opportunities to improve the targeting and monitoring of existing programs and ensure that their payment levels are adequate. The current system is predominantly paper-based and lacks a harmonized beneficiary registry. The time from enrollment to the program to payment of benefits can also be protracted (Government of Nauru 2022a).

To address these challenges, the National Social Protection Strategy aims to lift people out of poverty by reducing vulnerability and building resilience. The strategy aims to strengthen institutional capacity and the underlying administrative systems and processes to enable the existing system to be scaled up in response to shocks.

Promoting employment and an active labor market is one aspect of the strategy. To help address Nauru's high unemployment rate, particularly among young people, the strategy calls for training opportunities to upskill people and employment services, including those targeted at self-employment and entrepreneurs, such as by facilitating access to credit.

Expanding the coverage of social protection to new groups and increasing the level of benefits will inevitably raise government spending. Yet, even without a policy change, the cost of the aged pension is forecast to approximately double over the next 20 years because of an ageing population (Figure 8). In total, the strategy forecasts that government spending on social protection will rise from 4.1% of GDP in FY2021 to 6.0% in FY2041.

Ensuring adequate fiscal space to fund social protection will be a key policy challenge. Nauru's volatile and uncertain revenues, drawn mainly from external sources including the Regional Processing Centre (RPC) and fishing license fees, complicate an analysis of what the fiscally sustainable level of social protection will be in the future.[6] Although government revenues increased rapidly from FY2016 to FY2021, the RPC's transition to an "enduring capability" arrangement from January 2023 could entail a significant reduction in revenues over the medium term (Government of Nauru 2022b).

The National Social Protection Strategy recognizes that domestic resource mobilization is a major element in ensuring the long-term sustainability of social protection. Options such as expanding contributory schemes, broadening the tax base, and reallocating public expenditures could help ensure that reliable financing is available. The government plans to undertake fiscal analysis and develop a sustainable financing strategy for the National Social Protection Strategy to support long-term budget planning.

Outside of social protection, it is crucial to ensure that government spending on measures that are aimed at reducing hardship and cost-of-living pressures, such as the Nauru Community Housing scheme whose financing rose to 17.5% of GDP in FY022, and subsidies to state-owned enterprises to keep prices low, are likewise efficient and well-targeted.

The challenge of sustainably financing social protection will likely involve difficult decisions. But the social and economic benefits of implementing well-designed social protection programs that reduce vulnerability and cushion people against shocks are potentially high.

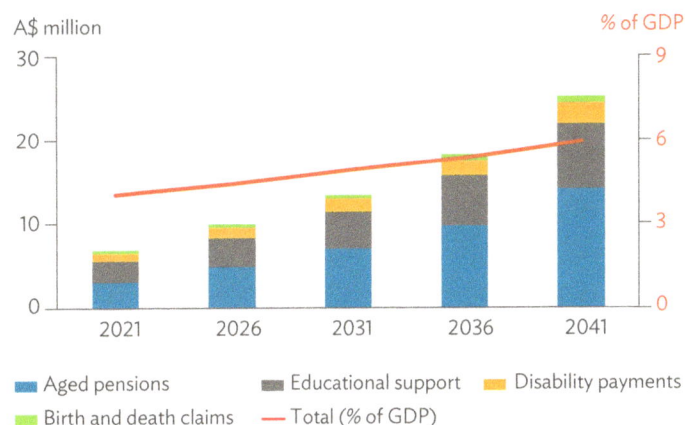

Figure 8: Projected Cost of Nauru's Social Assistance Programs

COVID-19 = coronavirus disease, GDP = gross domestic product.

Notes:

1. Years are fiscal years ending on 30 June of that year.

2. Data for 2021 differ from Figure 7 with the release of updated figures from the Government of Nauru.

3. Ex-gratia payments against the impacts of COVID-19 are not included.

4. Educational support includes back-to-school, Nauru Educational Assistance Trust (NEAT) scheme, and the school lunch program.

Source: Government of Nauru. 2022. *National Social Protection Strategy 2022–2032*. Yaren.

Endnotes

[1] The strategy was developed with technical and financial support from ADB and funding from the Ireland Trust Fund for Building Climate Change and Disaster Resilience in Small Island Developing States.

[2] The program started as a privately funded initiative in 2013 (Government of Nauru 2022a).

[3] In addition, a pension is available to former members of Parliament under the Parliamentary Pension Fund.

[4] There were about 6,960 people aged 18 and above in FY2021. In the 2012–2013 Household Income and Expenditure Survey, only 3% of households reported subsistence business income as their main source of income, while 1.8% reported home production consumed. On the other hand, 67.3% of households reported wage and salary income as their main source (Government of Nauru 2014).

[5]   The increase in social protection spending was faster than the overall rise in spending, with the ratio climbing from 3.1% of recurrent spending in FY2019 to 4.7% in FY2022. It is expected to rise further to 5.8% in FY2023.

[6]   From FY2018 to FY2022, RPC-related revenues accounted for 38% of total revenues and grants while fishing license fees accounted for 26%.

References

Government of Nauru. 2014. *Household Income and Expenditure Survey (HIES) 2012/2013*. Yaren.

Government of Nauru. 2016. *Nauru Education Assistance Trust Bill 2016*. Yaren.

Government of Nauru. 2021. *Republic of Nauru Department of Finance Annual Report 2020–21*. Yaren.

Government of Nauru. 2022a. *National Social Protection Strategy 2022–2032*. Yaren.

Government of Nauru. 2022b. *Republic of Nauru 2022–23 Budget: Budget Paper No. 1*. Yaren.

International Labour Organization (ILO). 2015. *Situational Analysis of Employment in Nauru*. Suva.

Pacific Community (SPC). 2022. *Stat of the week: It is estimated that 84.6% of people in Nauru living with a severe disability collect disability social protection benefits*. Noumea.

Building toward better social protection in Palau

Lead author: Rommel Rabanal, with inputs from Ninebeth Carandang

As one of the most tourism-driven economies not only in the Pacific but also globally, Palau has been among the hardest hit by the adverse economic and social impacts of the COVID-19 pandemic. Travel restrictions reduced tourist arrivals from close to 90,000 just prior to the pandemic to 41,753 in FY2020 (ended 30 September 2020) and further to just 3,407 in FY2021. As a result, the economy contracted sharply by a cumulative 26.1% during this 2-year period. Community transmission of COVID-19 in early 2022—along with rigidities in restoring flight connections with major source markets for tourists, destination competition with neighboring economies in Asia, and lingering uncertainties to the global tourism outlook—constrain the outlook for near-term recovery.

In response, the government delivered a comprehensive package of temporary relief measures, with budget support from ADB, as an immediate measure to mitigate hardship (ADB 2020). The Coronavirus Relief One-Stop Shop (CROSS) Program provided for unemployment assistance, temporary jobs, concessional loans for businesses, and expanded lifeline utility subsidies to help cushion the most severe socioeconomic impacts on affected businesses and workers during FY2020–FY2022 (OEK 2020b). In total, the CROSS Program benefited more than 2,500 employers and employees, including 1,645 who received unemployment benefits and 774 workers who were able to shift to temporary employment in the public and civil society sectors, among others, during the pandemic.

To supplement these temporary assistance and broad policy reform measures, the government and ADB also developed a grant project to support more targeted interventions toward building systems that will help strengthen the resilience of vulnerable groups over the longer-term. Experience during the pandemic underscored gaps in Palau's social protection space that contribute to heightened impacts on vulnerable sectors during episodes of extreme adverse shocks.

Social protection in Palau primarily involves social insurance, which provides direct benefits only to those in formal employment. Although the formal sector employs 83% of the labor force and generates 65% of household incomes, small-scale production of agricultural and marine products remains a key source of income for more than a third of Palauan households, including the most vulnerable (Figure 9) (Bureau of Budget and Planning 2015). Rising sea levels and saltwater inundation pose serious threats for many small agriculture producers in low-lying areas.

The government's formal social assistance expenditures in FY2015 were equivalent to about 0.7% of GDP, with limited assistance for wide swathes of vulnerable populations including older people and persons with disabilities (PWD). Senior citizens in Palau represent about 13% of the total population and this proportion is projected to rise steadily in coming years (Palau Red Cross Society 2020; OEK 2020a). Although 75% of older people are either employed or receive social security, many early retirees receive only modest payments (Office of Planning and Statistics 2015). The share of households headed by senior citizens without an income is highest in the population and urban centers of Babeldaob (54%) and Koror-Airai (27%), followed by outlying states (19%).

Further, even prior to COVID-19, there was a large unmet demand for support to address GBV. Latest estimates as of 2014 show that, from a sample of 6,503 women, 8% experienced domestic violence perpetuated by an intimate partner; 6% experienced violence perpetuated by a non-partner; and more than 14% were impacted by violence each year (Ministry of Health 2014). Despite this, only 90 cases are being reported to the police or judicial authorities every year (Palau Judiciary 2018 and Office of Planning and Statistics 2019). In 2012, Palau enacted the Family Protection Act, which seeks to address all forms of family violence, but a review of its implementation in 2017 identified service gaps including deficiencies in holistic case management support for family and GBV survivors. Amid COVID-19, anecdotal reports indicate increased incidence of domestic violence, with the number of cases reported to the police rising by more than 200% from March 2020 to July 2020.

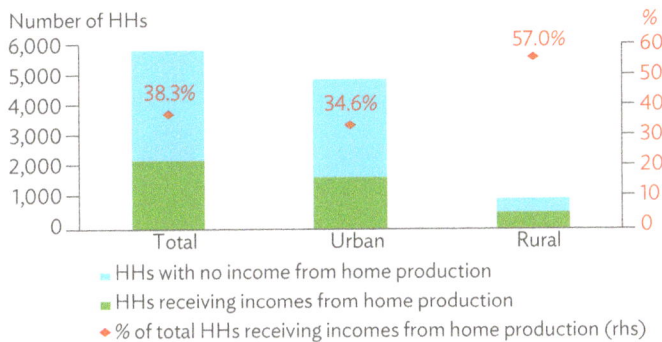

Figure 9: Households Receiving Incomes from Home Production in Palau

HH = household, rhs = right-hand scale.
Source: Government of Palau, Office of Planning and Statistics. 2015. *Republic of Palau: 2014 Household Income and Expenditure Survey*. Ngerulmud.

With cofinancing from the Asian Development Fund 13 thematic pool, the Japan Fund for Prosperous and Resilient Asia and the Pacific, and the Irish Trust Fund for Building Climate Change and Disaster Resilience in Small Island Developing States, ADB approved the COVID-19 Response for Affected Poor and Vulnerable Groups Project in August 2021 (ADB 2021). The project supports:

- **Food security.** In coordination with the Bureau of Agriculture and Palau Visitors Authority, the project is helping small agriculture producers, particularly women, to boost their outputs and incomes, including by promoting upland taro production. Support includes seedling grants, training and extension services, and establishment of a food processing facility. New products developed through the food processing facility will not only serve the domestic market but also supply the tourism sector, to help strengthen community–tourism linkages over the medium to long term.
- **Welfare of vulnerable groups.** The project is also supporting the government in delivering more holistic social protection services to older people and PWDs by providing community-based wellness promotion and gender-responsive case management services, including training for family and community caregivers. Assistance for home improvements and adaptations—along with development of home gardens—for healthy, safe, and accessible ageing-in-place is also being provided.
- **Multidisciplinary responses to mitigate GBV.** To help fill gaps in fully implementing the Family Protection Act, the project is developing an integrated case management support system for survivors, including a free 24-hour hotline, crisis counseling, and multisectoral referral pathways, while also rolling out a complementary social marketing campaign that raises awareness on GBV and informs stakeholders of available services and referral pathways. These will help improve help-seeking behavior and prevent domestic violence by gradually changing community social norms regarding GBV.

By 2024, the project aims to support: (i) at least 1,200 small agriculture producers, including 300 women, in expanding their production of taro; (ii) at least 150 homebound older persons and PWD, including 82 women, with holistic case management and wellness-promotion; (iii) community-wellness promotion activities; (iv) 100% of GBV survivors who seek help with case management support services; (v) 1,400 frontline workers with trainings on GBV; and (vi) at least 12,000 people through a social marketing campaign to help reshape community norms around GBV. As of November 2022, the case management and welfare services for homebound older persons have been ongoing. A total of 152 homebound older people has been visited to provide wellness services involving activities around music and arts, urban gardening, life coaching, and home improvements. GBV case management services are also available for GBV survivors and the project has partnered with the Belau Association of Non-Government Organizations to advance the social marketing campaign to combat GBV. Further, seed grants have been awarded to 18 women's groups across the states of Palau. In the coming months, the project's progress toward delivering its intended results can offer insights for the potential design, development, and refinement of similar social protection projects in other Pacific countries.

References

Asian Development Bank (ADB). 2020. Palau: Health Expenditure and Livelihoods Support Program. Manila.

ADB. 2021. Palau: COVID-19 Response for Affected Poor and Vulnerable Groups Project. Manila.

ADB. 2022. Palau: Recovery through Improved Systems and Expenditure Support Program (Subprogram 2). Manila.

Government of Palau, Bureau of Budget and Planning. 2015. *Census of Population, Housing, and Agriculture*. Ngerulmud.

Government of Palau, Ministry of Health. 2014. *Belau Family Health Survey*. Koror.

Government of Palau, Office of Planning and Statistics. 2015. *Republic of Palau: 2014 Household Income and Expenditure Survey*. Ngerulmud.

Government of Palau, Office of Planning and Statistics. 2019. *Palau Statistical Yearbook, 2019*. Koror.

Government of Palau. Palau Judiciary. 2018. *Court Annual Report 2018*. Koror.

Olbiil Era Kelulau (OEK). 2020a. *Republic of Palau Public Law No. 10-51: National Policy on Care for the Aging*. Ngerulmud.

OEK. 2020b. *Coronavirus Relief One-Stop Shop Act or CROSS Act, 2020 (Republic of Palau Public Law No. 10-56)*. Ngerulmud.

Palau Red Cross Society. 2020. *COVID-19 Household Assessment Report: Preliminary Results*. Koror.

Toward a social protection system in post–COVID-19 Papua New Guinea

Lead authors: Magdelyn Kuari and Marcel Schroder

Papua New Guinea (PNG) has a very limited national social protection system that supports the needs of vulnerable and disadvantaged individuals who face daily hardships through exposure to abuse, exploitation, negligence, and violence. Among this group are children (especially orphans but also adopted and fostered children), people with disabilities, landless people, widows, those who lose their jobs unfairly, and those living in acute poverty. Most households traditionally rely on informal protection mechanisms, involving shared land ownership and the extended family network. Strong ethnic group links (*wantok* system) provide risk-pooling and an informal social safety net through intercommunity support. However, this system is expected to weaken in urban and peri-urban areas with the expansion of the cash-based economy and fast population growth. Women, particularly those without access to land, are likely to be the most affected and vulnerable.

The lack of a social protection system constrained the government's support during the COVID-19 pandemic when the economy contracted in 2020 and 2021. Food security activities and funding assistance to smallholders in rural areas extended to only a few thousand households. While fiscal space is currently limited, rising resource revenues in the near term could help kick start social protection in PNG.

CURRENT STATE OF SOCIAL PROTECTION IN PNG

Despite its vast resource wealth, growth in PNG has often not been inclusive. According to the Medium Term Development Plan 3 (2018–2022), 52.5% of PNG's population was considered vulnerable and disadvantaged in 2016 and ADB estimates suggest that 26.8% of the population lived below the national poverty line in 2019.[1] Moreover, the formal sector in PNG remains tiny. In 2020, more than 85% of the population continued to rely on the informal sector for their livelihood (ADB 2020).

PNG does not have national unemployment benefits, or targeted benefits for the poor or households with children. One key constraint is a lack of administrative capacity to identify the vulnerable and disadvantaged and implement social protection programs. For example, the National Disaster Office is responsible for the provision of temporary relief and assistance during disasters in affected areas. The gaps in the emergency relief system were highlighted during the 2018 earthquake in Hela province because affected populations could only be reached days or, in some cases, weeks after the disaster. National identification registration has been ongoing since 2014, but allegations over misuse of funds and lack of project funding have hindered meaningful progress in several parts of the country, preventing the identification of individuals and groups in need of social protection programs.

In general, there is no clear and central coordination of social protection programs with subnational governments typically implementing their own programs. Funding for social protection interventions at the subnational government level is also not clearly reported, and there is no information on monitoring mechanisms.

In 2016, the government made substantial progress in adopting a National Policy on Social Protection (2015–2020), which included a strategy for integrated social protection. The final document's release in April 2016 was preceded by extensive consultations with communities, local governments, nongovernment organizations, and representatives of key vulnerable groups. Although the policy was a step forward, it remains relatively high-level, presenting objectives such as (i) to guide the development of sectoral policies, strategies, and plans on social protection, targeting initially vulnerable and disadvantaged groups; and (ii) to provide a guide for the development and implementation of specific program interventions on social protection in line with models, principles, and approaches advocated in the policy, targeting vulnerable and disadvantaged groups. Further, the social protection targets in the Medium-Term Development Plan 3 (2018–2022) aimed to reduce the dependency ratio[1] from 66.6% in 2016 to 50.0% by 2022, and the percentage of the population identified as vulnerable and disadvantaged reduced from 52.5% in 2016 to 30% by 2022, and to increase the proportion of children accessing protective services from 2.0% in 2013 to 25.0% by 2022.

SOCIAL PROTECTION PROGRAMS PROVIDED BY THE GOVERNMENT

Nonetheless, together with development partners, the national government provides some support including education fee assistance, family and child protection programs, legal aid services, parole service for prisoners, family support centers for victims of family and sexual violence, free provision of antiretroviral therapy for HIV/AIDS, free condoms and voluntary counselling test services, national voluntary services, and settlement upgrading (Department of Community Development and Religion 2016). There are government pension schemes for retired constitutional officeholders and support programs for people living with disability. The government also provides transport freight subsidy programs to support rural farmers. In May 2022, the government provided tax relief to low-income earners to mitigate high inflationary pressures stemming from global supply chain pressures and the economic fallout from the Russian invasion of Ukraine. There is limited research on how many households benefit from existing social protection programs. Available data from 2015 indicate that only 0.3% of intended beneficiaries are covered by support programs, much lower than in other Pacific island countries (ADB 2019).

FINANCING ISSUES

Since the commodity price boom in 2014, government revenue has declined substantially and budget deficits have widened, reaching the equivalent of 8.6% of gross domestic product in 2020 and 6.7% in 2021 (Figure 10). For 2022 and 2023, the government projects deficits of 5.9% and 4.4%, respectively (Department of Treasury 2022a). This has resulted in rising public debt (Figure 11), eroding fiscal space that is needed for financing future social protection programs.

Figure 10: Government of Papua New Guinea Budget Deficit

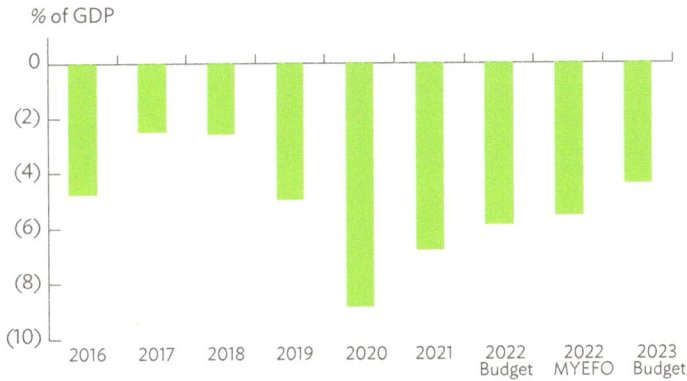

GDP = gross domestic product, MYEFO = Mid-Year Economic and Fiscal Outlook.
Sources: Government of Papua New Guinea, Department of Treasury. *National Budget, Volume 1, Economic and Development Policies*. Port Moresby (2 years: 2021–2022); Government of Papua New Guinea, Department of Treasury. 2022. *2022 Mid-Year Economic and Fiscal Outlook Report*. Port Moresby; and Government of Papua New Guinea, Department of Treasury. *Final Budget Outcome*. Port Moresby (6 years: 2016–2021).

Figure 11 : Papua New Guinea Debt

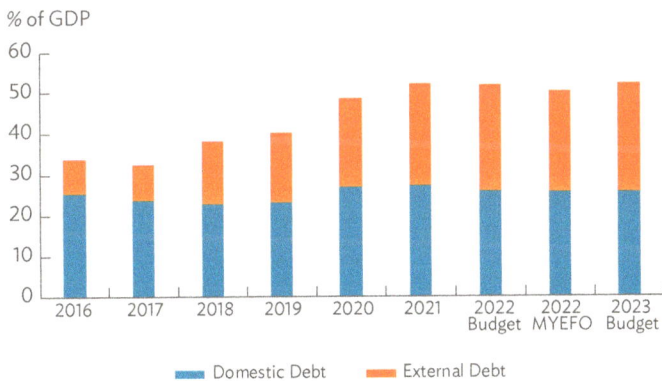

GDP = gross domestic product, MYEFO = Mid-Year Economic and Fiscal Outlook.
Sources: Government of Papua New Guinea, Department of Treasury. *National Budget, Volume 1, Economic and Development Policies*. Port Moresby (2 years: 2021–2022); Government of Papua New Guinea, Department of Treasury. 2022. *2022 Mid-Year Economic and Fiscal Outlook Report*. Port Moresby; and Government of Papua New Guinea, Department of Treasury. *Final Budget Outcome*. Port Moresby (6 years: 2016–2021).

The Department of Community Development and Religion, which is responsible for formulating and coordinating the implementation of social protection policy and programs in PNG, receives less than 0.5% of the annual national budget allocation. Actual spending by the department fell from K37.9 million in 2018 to K24.9 million in 2019, and remained under K30.0 million in 2021. Among other factors, this has affected the government's implementation of a disability policy that was approved in 2009. After some initial spending in 2010–2012, the policy has lost momentum amid a decline in government expenditure.

The government will need to raise revenue to finance an integrated national social protection system. In this regard, prospects for increased tax receipts from resource projects look promising in the coming years. As the amortization phase on financing loans of the PNG liquefied natural gas project ends, tax payments from the project are expected to surge from 2025 onwards. The reopening of the Porgera mine is also on the horizon, which will further increase government receipts. But even this year, there has been a sharp rise in resource revenue because PNG as a petroleum exporter benefited from spiking commodity prices following the Russian invasion of Ukraine. According to the government's 2022 Mid-Year Economic and Fiscal Outlook Report, resource revenue in 2022 will be K3.8 billion, K2.3 billion higher than estimated in the budget. However, this windfall is entirely allocated to additional recurrent expenditure instead of financing social protection programs.

CONCLUSION

Even as traditional forms of social insurance are weakening, PNG has made little progress in establishing a national social protection system, although the government formulated an implementation strategy in the National Policy on Social Protection (2015–2020). The updated version of the policy (2022–2030) is under review and will be for approval by the National Executive Council. The COVID-19 pandemic, through its negative impacts on health and economic livelihoods, has demonstrated the need for social protection to be ramped up to support the basic needs of the vulnerable and disadvantaged population. For this, the government needs to increase funding for social protection from a meager 0.5% of its annual budget allocation. The likely rise in resource revenues in the near term should be used for program financing. Social protection is a crosscutting issue and its mainstreaming in sectoral policies and programs of the government, including adequate resourcing, will be key to inclusive development in PNG.

Endnote

[1]   Defined as the proportion, per 100 of working-age population, of persons younger than 15 years old and older than 64.

References

Asian Development Bank (ADB). 2019. *The Social Protection Indicator for the Pacific: Assessing Progress*. Manila.

ADB. 2020. *Country Partnership Strategy: Papua New Guinea, 2021–2025*. Inclusive and Sustainable Growth Assessment (accessible from the list of linked documents in Appendix 3). Manila.

Government of Papua New Guinea, Department of Community Development and Religion. 2016. *National Policy on Social Protection*. Port Moresby.

Government of Papua New Guinea, Department of National Planning and Monitoring. 2017. *Medium Term Development Plan 3 (2018–2022)*. Port Moresby.

Government of Papua New Guinea, Department of Treasury. 2022a. *2022 National Budget, Volume 1, Economic and Development Policies*. Port Moresby.

Government of Papua New Guinea, Department of Treasury. 2022b. *2022 Mid-Year Economic and Fiscal Outlook Report*. Port Moresby.

Government of Papua New Guinea. 2020. *Papua New Guinea's Voluntary National Review 2020-Progress of Implementing the Sustainable Development Goals*. Port Moresby.

Far from socially distant: Remittances and migration in the time of COVID-19 in Samoa and Tonga

Lead author: James Webb

Remittances are an important part of household income and informal safety nets in Samoa and Tonga. The recent increase in remittances has been a key mitigating factor against the socioeconomic impacts of the COVID-19 pandemic. With the reopening of borders by Samoa and Tonga, labor migration has resumed, bringing with it the opportunity for further remittance growth. Labor mobility programs and diaspora links will continue to be central to the development of these countries. Migration has played a hugely important role, but comes with challenges that must be managed.

Compared to the 12 months that ended in March 2020 when borders closed, remittances in Samoa were 44.3% higher in the 12 months to September 2022 and 35.0% higher in the 12 months to June 2022 in Tonga. Despite the large uptick in inflation in 2022, even in real terms, remittances increased 26.7% in Samoa between FY2020 (ended 30 June 2020 for both Samoa and Tonga) and FY2022 and 29.9% in Tonga, resuming the upward trend in remittances growth that had slowed in FY2019 (Figure 12). While some of this increase may have been a transition from informal transfer mechanisms (such as hand-carrying cash across borders) to more formal mechanisms (like money transfer operators), the scale of the increase suggests a significant net increase.

Remittances reached the equivalent of 36.2% of GDP in Samoa and 41.1% in Tonga in FY2022. In nominal terms, across FY2021 and FY2022 combined, this equated to an additional $262.9 million in household income in Samoa and $238.6 million in Tonga, a far larger increase to household income than all other sources of nonwage income growth combined, including government COVID-19 support schemes. Clearly, remittances had a large moderating effect on the macroeconomic positions of both countries and avoided more serious economic declines.

Figure 12: Samoa and Tonga Personal Remittances ($ million)

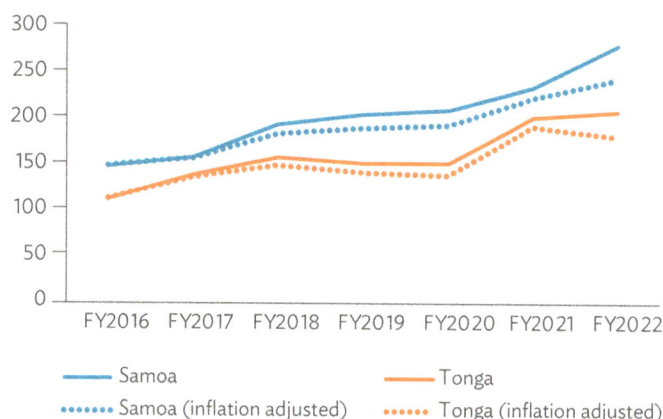

FY = fiscal year.
Note: Fiscal year ends 30 June of that year for Samoa and Tonga.
Sources: Central Bank of Samoa, National Reserve Bank of Tonga, and author calculations.

Figure 13: Samoa and Tonga Personal Remittances (% GDP)

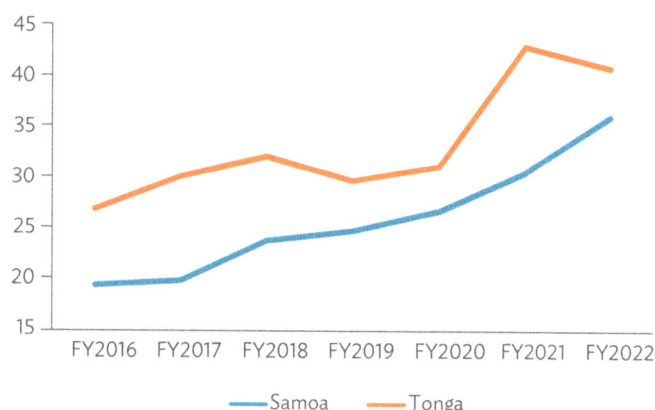

FY = fiscal year, GDP = gross domestic product.
Note: Fiscal year ends 30 June of that year for Samoa and Tonga.
Sources: Central Bank of Samoa, National Reserve Bank of Tonga, and author calculations.

Perhaps unsurprisingly, remittances were rated highly on household strategies to mitigate the impacts of COVID-19-induced economic shocks. The socioeconomic impact assessment of the United Nations for Samoa during the first year of the crisis estimated that 11% of households reported loss of job/livelihood because of COVID-19-related lockdown measures. This was felt most keenly by the active labor market groups of 26–45 years old (19% who reported job losses) and 46–65 years old (17% who reported job losses). For those people who reported a decline in income, the main coping strategies included farming/self-subsistence (40%), remittances (31%), and help from family/friends (30%)—noting that survey respondents could indicate more than one main strategy. Borrowing from banks (13%) or from family/friends (6%) was also significant, with government income assistance being the main strategy for only 2% of households. About 12% of respondents reported an increase in income, which was likely driven by the combination of remittances and government income support measures (such as an increase in social pensions for those over 65 years old).

This is likely consistent with experiences in Tonga, where remittances make up a significant portion of household income and have broad coverage. 54.0% of Tongan households in 2021 identified themselves as being recipients of remittances, with just over three-quarters (77.2%) of these households receiving transfers at least quarterly. More than half of households (56.2%) received them monthly and 38.2% of households have them as their main income source (2021 Census). Tonga Census data from 2021 show that the financial goals for remitting were mainly for daily needs, followed by home renovation/construction, vehicle purchases, or school costs. Survey data from Samoa support a similar prioritization, but also included loans. In both countries, contributions to the church, special events (*fa'alavelave* in Samoan or *me'a'ofa* in Tongan), and disaster assistance also ranked highly.

THE ROLE OF LABOR MOBILITY SCHEMES AND SHORT-TERM MIGRATION

While diaspora is well known to play a leading role in remittance flows, recent migration trends have also shown significant increases. For all categories of work visa (including labor programs, skilled visas, and bridging visas) to Australia and New Zealand, combined approvals for Tongans increased 63.6% between FY2019 and FY2022, and an incredible 295.2% for Samoans (Figure 14).

Figure 14: Total Work Visa Approvals (All Categories) in Australia and New Zealand

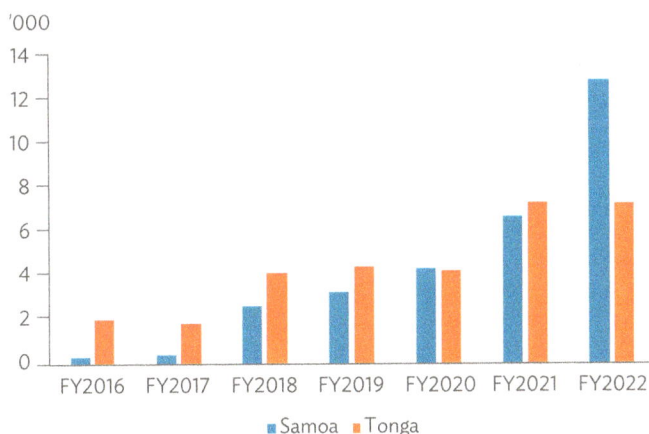

FY = fiscal year.
Note: Fiscal year ends 30 June of that year for Samoa and Tonga.
Sources: New Zealand data from MBIE Migration Data Explorer, and Australian data from Australian Department of Home Affairs. Temporary Visa Holders in Australia. (both accessed 8 November 2022).

Some of this rapid growth during the pandemic can be attributed to increased participation in labor mobility schemes: Australia's

Seasonal Worker Program (SWP) and Pacific Labour Scheme (PLS), which are now collectively referred to as the Pacific Australia Labour Mobility (PALM) scheme, and New Zealand's Registered Seasonal Employment (RSE) program.

With relatively high COVID-19 vaccination rates compared to other countries that are participating in these schemes, large diaspora links to the host countries, and facilitated travel arrangements during the closed border period, both Tonga and Samoa have been well-placed to participate in regional labor programs following the COVID-19 disruptions. When the numbers under the Australia and New Zealand schemes are combined, 5,182 Tongans and 7,622 Samoans were mobilized in-country by mid-2022—a 70% increase in the number of Tongans and more than double the total number of Samoans in the corresponding period in 2020. Only Vanuatu had more workers participating over the same time period (11,118).

Such is the size of the contributions to the regional mobility programs that the 2022 placements are rivaled only by the size of the public service in each country (6,578 in Tonga and 8,688 in Samoa), although all categories of temporary work visas easily exceed this level (7,283 for Tongans and 12,965 for Samoans). About 12% of the Samoan workforce in 2022 and 21.7% of Tongan households in 2021 participate in either the New Zealand or Australia labor programs. This has undoubtedly supported remittance flows, with estimates that as much as 90% of temporary workers sent about one-third of their total earnings back home. A study of Tongan migrants showed that RSE and SWP workers typically sent more money in remittances alone than they would have earned had they been working in Tonga, and PLS workers sent approximately the same as they would have earned at home. For Tongans living abroad, 25.6% of principal remitters in 2021 were from one of these labor programs.

Participation in labor programs continues to be dominated by males, though with notable impacts on domestic labor supply. In mid-2022, an estimated 18.2% of Tonga's male working-age population were engaged in labor mobility schemes. For Samoa, this was 14.1%. These percentages are notably higher than almost all other Pacific nations (Figure 15). This explains the complaint from some villages that they are struggling to find enough labor in certain sectors, such as agriculture and construction. For women, who still struggle to gain traction in the horticultural sector, the shares of local working-age populations were far lower, at only 3.7% for Tonga and 1.7% for Samoa. This has implications for the composition of domestic labor markets, with women playing an increasingly important role in the domestic workforce.

CAN REMITTANCES BE SUSTAINED?

It is difficult to predict the pathway that remittances will take in the near-term. Anecdotes of diaspora depleting cash savings or mortgaging assets to support families back home would clearly be unsustainable, but this prediction had been made for these countries before, with the outcome proving that the Samoa and Tonga diaspora are particularly resilient. Rapidly increasing inflation in both the home islands and host countries will undoubtedly increase pressure on both populations, but could be a motivating factor to further increase remittances in the short term to address the already high cost of living concerns back home (daily subsistence needs being a key concern for remitters).

Figure 15: Temporary Migrants in Australia or New Zealand

% of male working-age population

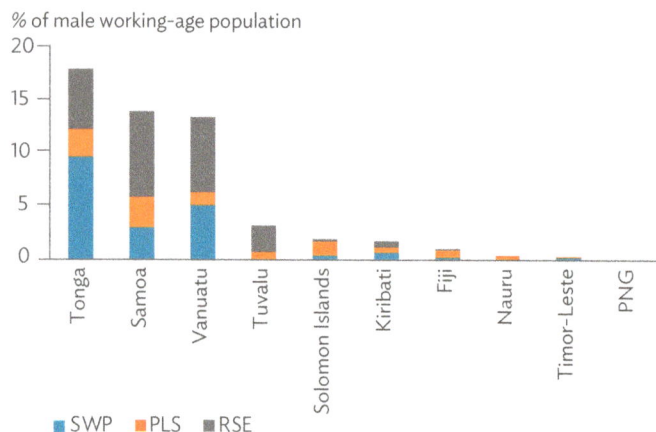

PLS = Pacific Labour Scheme (Australia), PNG = Papua New Guinea, RSE = Registered Seasonal Employment (New Zealand), SWP = Seasonal Worker Program (Australia).

Source: Howes, S., R. Curtain, and E. Sharman. 2022. Labour mobility in the Pacific: transformational and/or negligible? *Devpolicy Blog.*

Studies suggest that remittances often decay over time, as the links between diaspora and migrant community abroad with their home nations weaken (ADB 2005). Generally, two variables that appeared to influence the sustainability of remittances were the permanent residence status of the remitters in the host country and whether remitters still had immediate family in the home country. Having immediate familial ties (especially a parent) in the home country was a significant draw and could sustain remittances at high levels for extended periods. Length of absence from the home country was a less-significant factor in determining remittance decay. However, an increasingly significant motivating factor for migrants to remit is the accumulation of assets and investments at home, as well as maintaining familial and cultural ties. Certainly, this is the case for Samoa and Tonga, where remittances continue to climb year after year. What has distinguished Pacific island migrants, including Samoans and Tongans, is that they tend to stay in the host country even though they may have expressed an intention to return home (Macpherson 1994), and remittances can help reinforce a connection to their home islands.

However, second-generation migrants born in host countries are likely to send smaller amounts and only on demand. This suggests that maintaining remittance flows in the long run will depend on a steady flow of new migrant workers. While Samoan and Tongan diaspora communities have been particularly resistant to declining remittances at an individual level, the experience of the neighboring Cook Islands holds a cautionary tale. The Cook Islands diaspora living in New Zealand were traditionally a large source of remittances prior to the turn of the century. However, income flows have reversed. Not only are there now relatively few first-generation migrants (compared to second- and third-generation diaspora

communities), but there is a steady flow of capital to support school and university students abroad and outbound remittances from the extensive migrant labor force servicing the local tourism industry.

The opportunity for Cook Islanders to migrate freely to New Zealand and Australia reduced the barriers for families to unite across borders as well as the need for remittances—and likely accelerated these trends—but it represents a near-peer example of what may occur over the longer term in Samoa and Tonga if new migration slows or connections to the home islands weaken. Data on New Zealand's Pacific permanent residence visas certainly show that the demand from Samoans and Tongans to live permanently abroad is on a similar scale to that of Cook Islanders in earlier years. In 2019, 21% of all Samoans applied for the Pacific permanent residence visa in the hope of migrating to New Zealand, as compared to 7% of all Tongans (Curtain and Howes 2022). For both, the number of applicants exceeded the number of positions available by a factor of between 30 and 40 times the respective intakes. Up to 54% of Samoans said they were willing to permanently move to another country, confirming that the pathways to permanent migration are likely to be well subscribed, especially when familial units can qualify to be united through other visa categories. This may challenge the dominant role of remittances from diaspora as birth rates decline on home islands and subsequent generations of Samoans and Tongans are born overseas to complete family units.

OTHER CONSIDERATIONS FOR THE FUTURE OF REMITTANCES

In terms of providing ongoing social protection, remittances have clearly been important in mitigating the economic impacts of COVID-19 and will continue to play a central role in the economies of Samoa and Tonga. This will require a continued stream of labor moving to offshore markets. Recent statements by the Government of Samoa to review the role of migration are timely. Migration can be a source of continued benefit for individuals, the home countries, and vibrant diaspora communities. Consequently, there are areas that governments can work on that will ensure that remittances and migration continue to provide a social benefit:

- **Education, skills, and gender.** The focus of both Samoa and Tonga on education and skills of all workers is unambiguously beneficial to both individuals and the home countries, as is the aim to increase the number of women who are participating in migration programs. Both measures would reduce the asymmetrical gender impacts on local labor markets and social issues. Further, gender plays an important role in remittances. Data show that, virtually without exception, women tend to be more frequent remitters, remit for longer, look after family members with disabilities, and maintain wider family networks with home islands.

- **Improve financial inclusion and reduce costs.** Efforts to reduce the costs of remittances will help to ensure that individuals feel their incomes are well spent, and continuing efforts on financial inclusion within borders will contribute to reducing barriers between migrant workers, diaspora, and their families back home. Formal access to financial and digital services will improve access to formal government transfer schemes and emergency response, as well as facilitate remittances and transfers, strengthen anti-money laundering efforts, and potentially promote business formalization. This may improve business investment opportunities subsequently, especially if improved access is prioritized. However, shifts toward online platforms may continue to face challenges in equitable access unless gender gaps in information and communication technology access and financial inclusion are addressed.

- **Provide investment pathways for diaspora**. Improvements to the general investment climate may encourage migrants to become more active in domestic capital markets as saver-rentiers or direct investors, appealing to second and third generations from abroad as a viable option to bring funds onshore. Migrants are unlikely to risk their financial capital in an investment in the home economy if safer alternatives exist elsewhere, particularly in New Zealand or Australia which are more familiar to them.

- **Improve domestic social protection programs.** Remittances can sometimes be unevenly distributed with particular personal circumstances inviting social exclusion (e.g., divorce, separation, and absence seeking work). Migration can reflect not just the pull of prospective higher standards of living, but also the push of inadequate social support and lack of economic opportunity in villages. This leaves an important opportunity to improve formal government transfer schemes to provide consistent and reliable coverage of the weakest members of society such as older persons, young children, and people with disabilities. Both Tonga and Samoa have universal pension schemes, although other vulnerable populations are less covered by formal programs. Government-funded programs and superannuation schemes may become more important over time and will need to be adjusted in response to the lived experiences of communities on the ground.

References

Asian Development Bank. 2005. *Remittances in the Pacific: An Overview*. Manila.

Australia's Department of Foreign Affairs and Trade. 2016. *Informal social protection in Pacific Island countries—strengths and weaknesses*. Canberra.

Curtain, R. 2022. *Brain drain 1: a growing concern. Devpolicy Blog.*

Curtain, R. and S. Howes. 2022. *The Pacific Engagement Visa is going to be incredibly popular. Devpolicy Blog.*

Edwards, R., M. Dornan, D. Doan and T. Nguyen. 2022. *Three questions on Tongan remittances. Devpolicy Blog.*

Government of Samoa. *2016. Samoa Census of Households 2015/16*. Apia.

Government of Tonga. 2022. *Tonga Census of Households 2021: Preliminary Results.* Nuku'alofa.

Government of Tonga. 2017. *Household Income and Expenditure Survey 2015/2016: Full Report*. Nuku'alofa.

Howes, S., R. Curtain, and E. Sharman. 2022. *Labour mobility in the Pacific: transformational and/or negligible? Devpolicy Blog.*

Macpherson, C. 1994. Changing Patterns of Commitment to Island Homelands: A case study of Western Samoa. *Pacific Viewpoint* 17, pp. 83–116.

United Nations and Samoa Bureau of Statistics. 2021. *Samoa Socio Economic Impact Assessment*. Apia.

Expanding social protection beyond the provident fund in Solomon Islands and Vanuatu

Lead authors: Jacqueline Connell and Prince Cruz

Social protection in Solomon Islands and Vanuatu has focused on a contributory retirement and insurance scheme provided by their respective national provident funds (NPFs). Despite the potential benefits of expanding social protection, there are several challenges not least of which is the governments' limited fiscal space to increase expenditure in the wake of the COVID-19 pandemic. Thin public administration and information systems, combined with low financial inclusion, pose challenges to identifying vulnerable people and delivering assistance. This brief will discuss the social protection system in Solomon Islands and Vanuatu, efforts to expand support during the pandemic, and suggestions for the path forward.

The economic and social structures of Solomon Islands and Vanuatu suggest that social protection could play an important role to prevent and reduce poverty. Solomon Islands had the lowest income per person among Pacific developing member countries at $2,300 in 2020, while Vanuatu is not far off with $3,190 (ADB 2022). Both countries have young populations leading to relatively high dependency ratios, measured as the share of people that working-age adults must support. About one in three children is stunted because of undernutrition (page 36).

Households in both countries are also vulnerable to income shocks because of their susceptibility to disasters from natural hazards, such as cyclones, earthquakes, floods, and (for Vanuatu) volcanic eruptions. The WorldRiskReport 2021 ranked Vanuatu with the highest disaster risk out of 181 countries, followed by Solomon Islands.

Informal social networks, known locally as the *wantok* system, have traditionally provided social safety nets and enabled communities to pool risk. However, these traditional systems are often inadequate when a large disaster strikes. With COVID-19, households were initially able to rely on traditional safety nets but had to resort eventually to unsustainable coping strategies such as sale of assets or reduction of food consumption (World Bank 2022). The *wantok* system has also come under pressure from rising urbanization as people move away from their local community, often in search of jobs (Nanau and Labu-Nanau 2021). Population density in Honiara, the capital of Solomon Islands, is now the highest in the Pacific, having risen from 3,343 people per square kilometer in 2009 to 5,950 in 2019 (ADB 2021).[1] The weakening of the *wantok* system is also observed in Vanuatu and Papua New Guinea (page 26).

Solomon Islands and Vanuatu do not have government-funded social assistance programs for the unemployed, people with disabilities, single parents, or elderly people. While the governments responded promptly to the COVID-19 pandemic with economic stimulus packages, they did not have existing social assistance systems from which to roll out support to vulnerable households.

COVID-19 RESPONSES

As part of the Economic Stimulus Program announced in May 2020, the Government of Solomon Islands provided support to farmers and small and medium-sized enterprises (SMEs). Financial support was distributed directly to applicants and through churches, schools, and local leaders. Five state-owned enterprises also benefited from subsidies to retain employees. Workers who were laid off because of COVID-19 were allowed to make a partial withdrawal from their Solomon Islands National Provident Fund (SINPF) contributions to cushion the income shock.

For Vanuatu, the government has launched three stimulus packages since 2020 with support for formal sector workers and businesses through the Employment Stabilization Scheme and the SME Grants. However, only Vanuatu National Provident Fund (VNPF) members and registered firms with active contributions have been allowed to access the employment scheme. VNPF members affected by COVID-19 were also allowed to take hardship loans, of which 2,242 were approved as of March 2022, utilizing Vt50 million of the allocated Vt300 million (Roberts 2022a).

A report by the Government of Vanuatu (2021) indicates some of the challenges involved with delivering support to beneficiaries and processing payments for the stimulus packages. These include incomplete documentation, lack of bank accounts, and incomplete VNPF contributions.

ROLE OF THE NATIONAL PROVIDENT FUNDS

As the pandemic-related stimulus packages conclude, the NPFs, which provide a compulsory savings and retirement scheme, have returned to being the main providers of formal social protection.

Under the NPFs, workers are required to save a portion of their income to withdraw upon retirement, death, disability, or job redundancy. Partial drawdowns are allowed for those affected by medical emergencies or calamities, such as cyclones or droughts (and social unrest in the case of Solomon Islands), upon approval by the government. While partial withdrawals can help people bounce

back from unexpected shocks, they clearly come at the cost of reducing workers' retirement savings.

As the retirement benefit is limited to a one-time lump sum withdrawal of contributions, the NPFs offer limited support to sustain consumption after retirement. Lump-sum benefits can be vulnerable to pressures for speedy consumption and the ILO (2006a; 2006b) noted that this is exacerbated when community and family obligations are as strong as they are in Solomon Islands and Vanuatu.

Since 2007, contributions of VNPF members have been divided into a retirement account (50%), an investment account (25%), and a medi-save account (25%). Partial withdrawals can only be done against the investment account (for calamities) or the medi-save account (for medical emergencies), leaving the retirement account intact.

Contributions to the SINPF are equivalent to 12.5% of the employee's salary (5% from the employee and 7.5% paid by the employer). For the VNPF, contributions are equivalent to 8% with 4% deducted from the employee's salary and 4% paid by the employer.

Although the NPFs help to save for unexpected shocks and retirement, their coverage has been largely limited to formal sector workers. Only about 32% of Solomon Islanders aged 15 and over were registered members of SINPF with credit balances in 2019.[2] Members with credit increased from 122,383 in 2015 to 145,977 in 2021 (Figure 16). The total balance of members' contributions was equivalent to about 27.0% of GDP (or SI$3.5 billion) in 2021.

Figure 16: Solomon Islands National Provident Fund Members

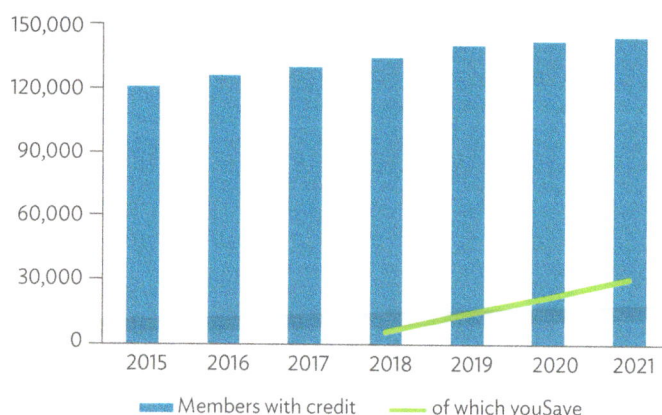

Note: Members with credit balance are those with existing contributions in the fund which are entitled to the annual crediting interest rate.
Sources: Solomon Islands National Provident Fund Annual Report (various years), and Central Bank of Solomon Islands.

In Vanuatu, about 44% of the eligible population were VNPF members in 2020 (80,412 of the 184,252 people aged 15 and older) (Figure 17). Annual contributions slightly dipped in 2020 because of the pandemic, but recovered to Vt2.5 billion in 2021 (Roberts 2022b). The total balance of VNPF members' funds was equivalent to about 20.0% of GDP (or Vt21.4 billion) in 2019.

Figure 17: Vanuatu National Provident Fund Members and Contributions

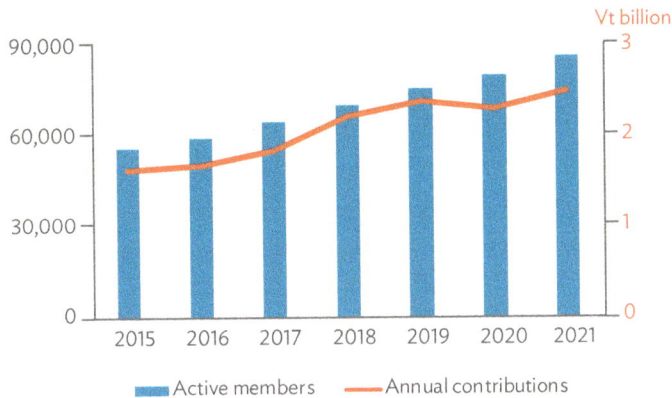

Sources: Vanuatu National Provident Fund Annual Report (various years), and Reserve Bank of Vanuatu.

in 2019. The Solomon Islands' National Women's Financial Inclusion Policy 2022–2026 (CBSI 2022) is a clear step in the right direction.

Figure 18: Solomon Islands National Provident Fund Members, by Age Group and Gender, 2019

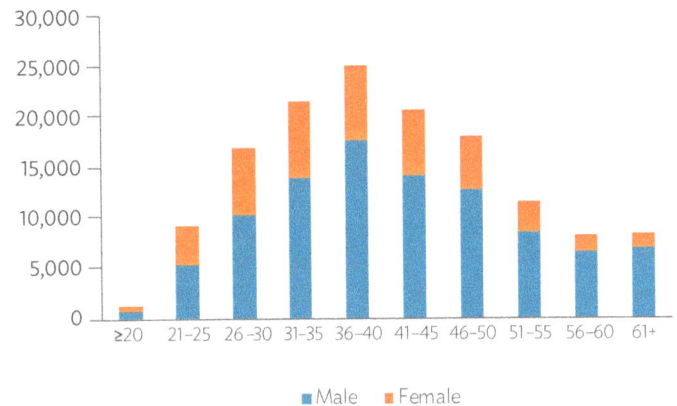

Note: Members with credit balance.

Source: Solomon Islands National Provident Fund 2019 Annual Report.

Until recently, informal workers have lacked access to the NPFs, leaving them in a vulnerable position during retirement. This particularly impacted women who have lower labor force participation rates and are more likely to be involved in informal work (Cruz and Ilala).[3]

However, positive steps have been taken to expand access to the funds, resulting in increased membership. In Solomon Islands, the voluntary savings scheme, youSave, was introduced by the SINPF in 2017 (CBSI 2017). The scheme targets self-employed and informal sector workers (including market vendors, farmers, and taxi drivers). Using digital innovations, membership has grown rapidly and reached 31,067 members in 2021 (up from less than 6,000 in 2018), of which 53% were women. Partnering with two mobile network operators, youSave members can buy airtime load from their nearest mobile agent and seamlessly convert the load into an SINPF contribution (IMF 2022a). In Vanuatu, the VNPF allowed informal sector workers to join as voluntary members in 2019. In 2021, there were more than 3,000 voluntary members, up from 888 in 2019 members (Roberts 2022b).[4]

CONSIDERATIONS FOR THE PATH FORWARD

Turning to the future, governments and development partners have a role to play in cushioning people from income shocks and supporting vulnerable people. Social safety nets may promote social stability and strengthen public support for reforms that are needed for macroeconomic stability and sustainable growth (IMF 2022b). When considering how to improve or expand the social protection system, there are several issues to consider.

First, sustainable financial management of the provident funds will help ensure that they support members into the future. In Solomon Islands, the CBSI is reviewing the SINPF Act and reforms will likely be needed to ensure that the SINPF functions as a modern and efficient funds management operation, and to remove barriers to women's participation. Women comprised less than a third of SINPF members, which reflects their low share in formal, paid employment (Figure 18).[5] In Vanuatu, women accounted for only 38% of members

Second, ensuring that new social safety net programs are well targeted to vulnerable groups will help ensure the greatest impact for a given cost. Data from the Vanuatu National Sustainable Development Plan Baseline Survey for 2019–2020 indicate that children and the elderly have higher hardship rates than working-age people (VNSO 2021). The hardship rate was highest at 21.8% for those aged 70 and above, followed by those aged 11–20 at 18.3% and those aged 0–10 at 17.2% (Figure 19).[6] Introducing social safety nets for these groups may help reduce hardship and avoid problems associated with social assistance that discourages work, given that children and the elderly fall outside the working-age population.

Figure 19: Vanuatu Hardship Rate, by Age Group

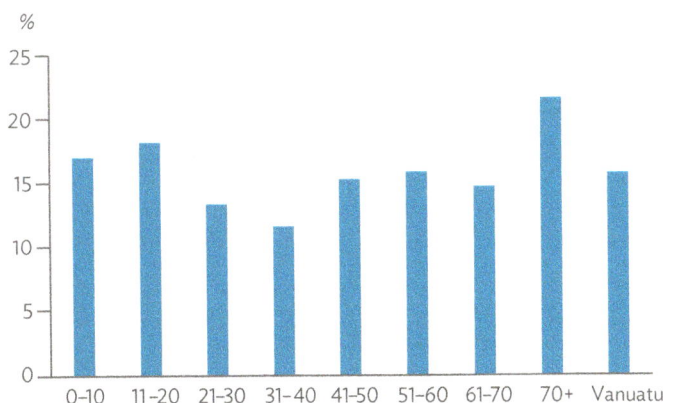

Note: Hardship rate refers to the percentage of population who are living below the national poverty line.

Source: Vanuatu National Statistics Office. 2021. *Hardship in Vanuatu: 2019–2020 Vanuatu National Sustainable Development Plan Baseline Survey*. Port Vila.

Third, ensuring that labor mobility programs are well designed can support the role of remittances to provide an alternate income source and safety net for households (page 28). Government labor assistance programs are largely limited to support for seasonal workers bound for Australia and New Zealand. To maximize the benefits, it is crucial to ensure that labor mobility assistance programs support former seasonal workers to reintegrate to the local labor market upon return and ensure that their skills are used and shared with other workers. As part of the reintegration efforts, a pilot program was launched in 2020 allowing Ni-Vanuatu seasonal workers in New Zealand to contribute into their VNPF accounts (Bedford 2021).

Fourth, increasing financial inclusion in rural areas may improve the targeting and delivery of potential new social safety nets. For instance, only 30% of adults in rural areas in Vanuatu have bank accounts as against 56% for urban residents (VNSO 2017). Innovative solutions are needed to overcome the challenges of the dispersed populations and scattered geography of Solomon Islands and Vanuatu (page 37). Improving internet connectivity can help tremendously to achieve this. In Vanuatu, informal sector workers, many of whom are self-employed, have been able to access social security services through mobile phone technology since 2021 (ILO 2021). The Vanuatu National Financial Inclusion Strategy 2018–2023 targets that an additional 54,000 (total of 130,000) adults will be active users of formal or semiformal financial services by 2023, of which 50% will be women (RBV 2018).

Finally, ensuring that new social protection programs are fiscally sustainable will help avoid crowding out other development spending. Expenditure projections of new programs should be incorporated into a medium-term fiscal framework. Mobilizing more sustainable sources of revenue can also create fiscal space for the government to respond to economic shocks and expand social protection. In Solomon Islands, the Parliament passed the Tax Administration Act in 2022 and there are plans to introduce a broad-based value-added tax. In Vanuatu, the government appointed the National Revenue Governance Committee in 2021 to develop policy options to broaden the revenue base.

Endnotes

[1] Population density in Honiara was also significantly higher than the national average of 24 persons per square kilometer (Government of Solomon Islands 2020).

[2] In 2019, there were 192,680 registered SINPF members, but only 74% were with credit balance, i.e., those with existing contributions that are entitled to the annual crediting interest rate. The Central Bank of Solomon Islands (CBSI) uses SINPF active contributors as proxy for formal employment. In June 2022, active contributors were at 55,812, down from 60,643 in December 2019, according to the CBSI quarterly bulletin. ILO (2006a) stated that, in 2002, there were 113,655 SINPF members but 57,903 were inactive (implying 55,752 active members). Despite the 78% increase in population, active contributors were relatively flat for 2 decades.

[3] Further, the ADB-UN Rapid Gender Assessment of the impact of COVID-19 found that more women in Solomon Islands were pushed into the informal sector as a result of the COVID-19 pandemic (UNWOMEN and ADB 2022).

[4] Voluntary members were just 3% of total contributing members in 2021, which indicates that majority of informal sector workers remains outside the VNPF.

[5] In the Solomon Islands' 2009 census, the labor force is roughly equally divided between males and females, but only 33% of paid workers were females. Similarly in the 2017 agricultural census, only 33% of public and private employees were female (while 59% of unpaid workers were female).

[6] Hardship rate refers to the percentage of population who are living below the national poverty line set at Vt147,944 (around 42% of GDP per capita in 2020). The hardship rate for the urban population (Port Vila and Luganville) was at 2%, compared to 21% of the rural population (VNSO 2021).

References

Asian Development Bank (ADB). 2021. *Asian Development Outlook 2021: Financing a green and inclusive recovery*. Manila (April).

ADB. 2022. *Basic Statistics 2022*. Manila (April).

Bedford, C. 2021. Supporting NZ's seasonal workers to remit and save. *Devpolicy Blog* (24 March).

Bündnis Entwicklung Hilft. 2021. *WorldRiskReport 2021: Focus Social Protection*.

Central Bank of Solomon Islands (CBSI). 2017. *What NPF's new saving scheme is*. Honiara.

CBSI. 2022. *National Women's Financial Inclusion Policy 2022–2026*. Honiara.

Cruz, P. and D. Ilala. 2021. Level up: raising the quality of labor in Solomon Islands. *Pacific Economic Monitor*. Manila: ADB (July).

Government of Solomon Islands. 2020. *Honiara city population growth a concern*. Honiara.

Government of Solomon Islands. 2022. *The 2022 Budget Speech: Building Our Resilience: Laying Strong Foundation for Growth*. Honiara.

Government of Vanuatu, Department of Finance and Treasury. 2021. *Stimulus package*. Port Vila.

International Labour Organization (ILO). 2006a. *Social Protection for All Men and Women: A sourcebook for extending social security coverage in Solomon Islands – options and plans*. Suva.

ILO. 2006b. *Social Security for All Men and Women: A sourcebook for extending social security coverage in Vanuatu – options and plans.* Suva.

ILO. 2021. *Digitalization enables 2,000 informal sector workers access social security.* 19 October.

International Monetary Fund (IMF). 2022a. 2021 Article IV Consultation-Press Release; Staff Report; and Statement by the Executive Director for Solomon Islands. Washington, DC.

IMF. 2022b. *IMF Engagement on Social safety Net Issues in Surveillance and Program Work.* Washington, DC.

Nanau, G. L. and M. Labu-Nanau. 2021. *The Solomon Islands' Social Policy Response to Covid-19: Between Wantok and Economic Stimulus Package.* CRC 1342 No. 18. Covid-19 Social Policy Response Series.

Reserve Bank of Vanuatu (RBV). 2018. *Vanuatu National Financial Inclusion Strategy 2018–2023.* Port Vila.

Roberts, A. 2022a. 2,232 VNPF hardship loans approved. *Vanuatu Daily Post* (26 March).

Roberts, A. 2022b. VNPF collects Vt2b contribution, Vt1b revenue. *Vanuatu Business Review* (22 January).

UNWOMEN and ADB. 2022. *Two years on, The lingering gendered effects of the COVID-19 pandemic in Solomon Islands.*

Vanuatu National Statistics Office (VNSO). 2017. *2016 Post Pam Mini Census Report, Vol 1.* Port Vila.

VNSO. 2021. *Hardship in Vanuatu: 2019–2020 NSDP Baseline Survey.* Port Vila.

World Bank. 2022. COVID-19 in Solomon Islands-Economic and Social Impacts: Insights from the January-February 2022 round of high frequency phone surveys. Washington, DC.

POLICY BRIEFS

Seven future directions for social protection in the Pacific

Pacific developing member countries (DMCs) face not only significant challenges but also unique opportunities to channel the impacts of the coronavirus disease (COVID-19) pandemic into strategies that will build resilience and lead to development. Some of these DMCs are confronting fragile contexts,[1] and new social protection initiatives offer prospects to strengthen government service delivery and consolidate social contracts that build state credibility and reinforce demand for good governance. The Pacific's most promising social protection directions will better enable governments to invest in human and cognitive capital, develop productive opportunities for youth, and optimize a mix of climate and development strategies that will build green and sustainable societies and economies. This policy brief maps out seven future directions for social protection in Pacific DMCs, documenting trends in successes and identifying critical areas for future progress.

IMPROVING COVERAGE OF VULNERABLE GROUPS

A positive trend and future direction for social protection in the Pacific involves the progressive expansion of coverage to vulnerable groups. Pacific DMCs have expanded social pensions, disability grants, child benefits, and other programs to cover more of the population. Discussions with policy makers and key stakeholders in the subregion indicate that this trend is likely to continue as a response to climate change and disaster risks, and how COVID-19 exacerbated difficulty and vulnerability to a scale not previously experienced by the subregion.

In the past 15 years, the Cook Islands, Fiji, Nauru, Tonga, and Tuvalu have adopted social protection schemes for people with disabilities, while the Cook Islands, Fiji, Kiribati, Nauru, Niue, and Samoa have implemented universal old-age pensions (Pacific Disability Forum 2018). Fiji plans to expand social protection support for vulnerable groups because its latest national development plan indicates that "targeted social protection will continue to be provided for the vulnerable through new initiatives" (Government of Fiji 2017). Indeed, with support from the Government of Australia, it has expanded social assistance benefits to tackle vulnerability, building on commitments entrenched in its national disability and gender policies (Fiji National Council for Disabled Persons and Government of Fiji 2008; Government of Fiji 2014). Tonga has also improved the shock-responsiveness of its national disability benefit scheme, expanding benefits in the aftermath of Cyclone Gita (Larasati et al. 2019). Tonga also increased social pension benefit to those aged 80 years and older (Socialprotection.org). These benefits proved vital in strengthening resilience to the economic consequences of the COVID-19 pandemic (UNPRPD 2020).

INVESTING IN EARLY CHILDHOOD DEVELOPMENT

An important area of social protection involves investments in early childhood development—a complex intersectoral initiative that includes social protection, health, education, water and sanitation, care practices, and child protection. Young children in the Pacific face high rates of malnutrition, which has resulted in high rates of stunting (UNICEF 2018). The pattern of under-five stunting rates[2] reflects the need for key investments in early childhood nutrition in several Pacific DMCs (Figure 1).

Figure 1: Stunting Rates of Children under Age 5 Years in the Pacific (%)

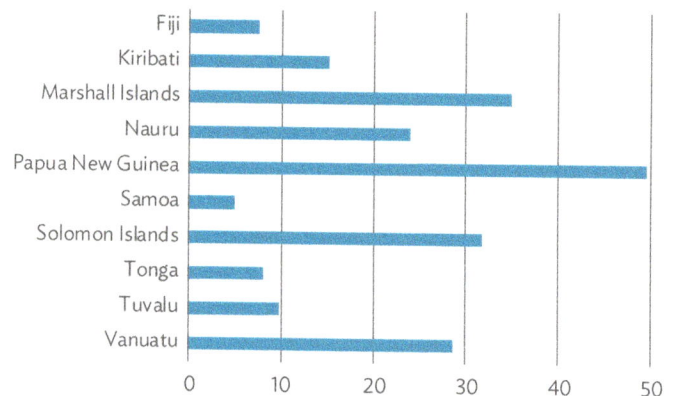

Source: United Nations Children's Fund. Early Childhood Development (accessed 12 May 2022).

The demographics of Pacific DMCs—with falling birth rates, rising life expectancy, and high rates of emigration—intensify the challenge of rising dependency ratios (see page 27, endnote 1 for a definition), which increasingly require higher growth rates of labor productivity to lift living standards. Recognizing this, governments across the subregion have elevated the role of child-sensitive social protection investments, particularly focusing on early childhood development. These investments have been identified as among the highest-yielding initiatives that support future economic growth and prosperity (Hoddinott et al. 2013) and they build cognitive capital that aligns economic growth and development strategies with economic opportunities (Samson, Fajth, and Francois 2016).

EXPANDING PROMOTIVE SOCIAL PROTECTION WITH A FOCUS ON YOUTH

A life-cycle approach to social protection also includes a focus on youth development. Pacific DMCs will benefit from social protection initiatives that strengthen livelihoods and employment, and youth represent the main beneficiaries from such directions since they face high unemployment rates. Social protection works to enhance youth opportunities—starting with investments in cognitive capital in early childhood, continuing with programs that complement educational achievement, and leading to specific initiatives that support a transition to more productive livelihoods.

Fiji's national development plan emphasizes "empower[ing] Fijians so that they may graduate out of poverty" (Government of Fiji 2017). It indicates that social protection should support education, pregnant women in rural areas, and other initiatives that build the long-term capabilities of the labor force. This includes expanding numbers for youth development programs, including empowerment and training initiatives with a focus on entrepreneurship, leadership, and tackling challenges associated with climate change.

RECOGNIZING THE VITAL ROLE OF INCLUSIVE DIGITAL TECHNOLOGIES

Pacific DMCs are recognizing the potential for inclusive digital technologies, not only to improve social protection delivery systems but also to expand livelihood opportunities for the subregion. Similarly, investing in childhood skills development increases the potential for inclusive digital technologies to contribute to development. Governments across the subregion are integrating these opportunities into their social protection systems and their larger development frameworks.

For example, Samoa 2040 recognizes that "digital technologies can act to stimulate business opportunities in e-commerce and e-services, as well as increas[e] productivity and growth in more traditional sectors such as agriculture and tourism." (Government of Samoa 2021) The vision identifies that "the government needs to...boost education, skills, and digital literacy" outcomes that a comprehensive social protection system can support.

Similarly, Fiji's national development plan highlights inclusive digital infrastructure, digital banking, and digitalization in climate response and governance. Indeed, Fiji has been providing exemplary digital responses to the COVID-19 pandemic; the government and Fiji National Provident Fund have employed digital payment mechanisms to deliver COVID-19 assistance, providing options for mobile phone money transfer service through Vodafone, Inkk, Digicel, or Post Fiji (Danford 2020). While the government paid the initial emergency COVID-19 cash transfers to street vendors and other affected workers directly through their bank accounts, it has provided subsequent benefits through a mobile money platform, finding that this significantly lowers delivery costs (UNDP and UN Women 2021). Such mobile technology also supports social distancing and other public health measures including contact tracing, and the Ministry of Communications negotiated with Vodafone and Digicel for free data allocations.

While governments around the world have invested in improving digital social protection systems to build resilience, Pacific DMCs have also begun to leverage inclusive technologies to improve social insurance and social assistance programs. For example, the Vanuatu National Provident Fund partnered with the International Labour Organization (ILO) and the United Nations Capital Development Fund and worked with Vodafone to launch M-Vatu, a payment gateway that enables informal sector workers, including the self-employed, to access social security services through their mobile phones. The ILO has planned similar initiatives in Fiji and Tonga (ILO 2021). The Pacific subregion relies heavily on provident funds as contributory mechanisms, which are more administratively intensive compared to noncontributory cash transfer programs. A focus on inclusive digital technologies can provide the necessary access to ensure that mobile payment gateways can support expansions of these mechanisms to the most vulnerable.

DEVELOPING NATIONAL SOCIAL PROTECTION STRATEGIES

In 2009, a subregional review of social protection found that no Pacific DMC had developed or implemented a national social protection policy or strategy that tackled deprivation and vulnerability (AusAID 2009). Many countries have resisted conventional notions of poverty, recognizing instead that some households faced "hardship" (Costella and Ivaschenko 2015). The COVID-19 pandemic—with both its devastating economic impacts as well as its foreshadowing of future crises—has accelerated governments' adoption of formal plans that document social protection commitments and approaches. The success of responses to the pandemic has demonstrated to governments and development partners that the potential of social protection will not only strengthen shock-responsive systems but also reinforce the social dimension of the new mix of climate, development, and equity strategies that are required for a transition to a green and sustainable society.

Global and regional development partners are providing resources and expertise that support this initiative. The Asian Development Bank (ADB) is supporting the development of national social protection policies or strategies in Papua New Guinea and Nauru (see page 22). The United Nation's Joint SDG Fund is providing technical assistance to the Cook Islands, Niue, Samoa, and other Pacific DMCs, including support to develop national social protection policy frameworks.

INTEGRATING COMPREHENSIVE SOCIAL PROTECTION PROGRAMMING THAT STRENGTHENS DEVELOPMENT

The trend toward formalizing national social protection policies and strategies enables and reinforces another vital direction: the increasing integration of more comprehensive social protection programming. While not all Pacific DMCs are planning to develop separate national social protection frameworks, many have incorporated key elements of more comprehensive strategies into their national development plans and visions. For example, Fiji does not have a national social protection policy or strategy but the national development plan substantively addresses social assistance schemes, affordable housing, gender equality, the inclusion of persons with disabilities, and climate change. Discussions with experts have highlighted the importance of robust data to support complex social protection programming. To strengthen this, the Pacific Statistics Methods Board is assessing the incorporation of modules into each Pacific DMC's main household income and expenditure survey to gather data on the impact of climate change on livelihoods and social welfare (SPC 2021).

OPTIMIZING THE MIX OF CLIMATE, DEVELOPMENT, AND EQUITY GOALS

Integrated and comprehensive social protection systems offer potential for tackling challenges posed by climate change. In addition, policy makers increasingly recognize that social protection offers a flexible instrument that better enables successful climate change mitigation and adaptation strategies. As disasters triggered by natural hazards become more frequent and severe—and the most vulnerable groups often bear a disproportionate share of the cost—Pacific DMCs need to gradually integrate social protection responses into comprehensive systems for disaster risk management and climate change adaptation.

Governments and development partners can do more to integrate climate and development priorities into their development plans and strategies. Today, shock-responsive approaches influence every aspect of social protection systems, demonstrating the importance of anticipatory actions that ensure the necessary mechanisms are in place before crisis strikes. ADB's new subregional strategy, *Pacific Approach, 2021–2025*, motivated in part by the increasing frequency and intensity of climate shocks, adopts a comprehensive approach that integrates social protection system support with initiatives to strengthen public and private sector responses to shocks (ADB 2021). The global COVID-19 crisis has tested national and global approaches and identified shortcomings that portend catastrophe in the face of the greater shocks that climate change threatens. Pacific DMCs and their development partners will increasingly rely on social protection's potential to help optimize the mix of climate, development, and equity strategies.

CONCLUSIONS

Over the next few decades, Pacific DMCs stand to benefit from realizing the full potential of developing comprehensive and integrated social protection systems that strengthen inclusive social development and equitable economic growth across the subregion. Social protection systems had been expanding steadily even prior to the COVID-19 crisis, and the pandemic's system of cascading and interacting shocks has demonstrated the universality of vulnerability and accelerated the adoption of social assistance, social insurance, and labor market programs The recent crisis has demonstrated the limits of Pacific traditional systems and reinforced governments' commitments to reach vulnerable groups, particularly older persons and persons with disabilities. Importantly, Pacific DMCs have increasingly focused on social protection investments in early childhood development, building the foundation for human and cognitive capital that drives future prosperity. Similarly, social protection initiatives have focused on harnessing the demographic dividend by promoting youth development and opportunities.

These expanded commitments to social protection contribute to a larger system for managing risk that will better enable Pacific DMCs to optimize a mix of climate and development strategies. Pacific DMCs are increasingly formalizing their commitments with national social protection policies and strategies. These frameworks produce vital synergies, enabling climate and development policies to work better together by (i) enabling people to better manage the entire life cycle of risks associated with the transitions that mitigating climate change will require, and (ii) providing Pacific DMCs with flexible tools for improving the equity impacts of the sometimes painful and costly adjustments that sustainable development strategies may need. Social protection provides Pacific DMCs with the pro-poor comprehensive and integrated climate and development policy frameworks, promising to support a future of inclusive social development and equitable economic growth.

Lead authors: Michael Samson (director, Economic Policy Research Institute) with inputs from Ninebeth Carandang (principal social development specialist, ADB) and Michiel Van der Auwera (former senior social development specialist, ADB). The policy brief is based on the forthcoming publication *The Social Protection Indicator for the Pacific–Tracking Development in Social Protection*.

Endnotes

[1] Fragility is the combination of exposure to risks and insufficient coping capacities of the state, system, and/or communities to manage, absorb, or mitigate those risks. Risks include, but are not limited to, weak governance and political instability, exposure to climate- or natural hazard-driven events, or exogenous economic shocks.

[2] Defined as the percentage of children aged 0–59 months whose height for age is below minus two standard deviations (moderate and severe stunting) and minus three standard deviations (severe stunting) from the median of the World Health Organization Child Growth Standards.

References

Asian Development Bank (ADB). 2010. Weaving Social Safety Nets. *Pacific Studies Series.* Manila.

ADB. 2021. ADB Generally Endorses New Strategy for Pacific Small Island Developing States. News release. 30 June.

Australian Agency for International Development (AusAID). 2009. Social Protection in the Pacific: Scoping Report. Unpublished.

Costella, C. and O. Ivaschenko. 2015. Integrating Disaster Response and Climate Resilience in Social Protection Programs in the Pacific Island Countries. *Social Protection and Labor Discussion Papers* No. 1507. Washington, DC: World Bank.

Danford, I. 2020. Total of $13.95M paid out so far by FNPF and the government through the COVID-19 withdrawal assistance. *Fiji Village.* 21 April.

Fiji National Council for Disabled Persons and Government of Fiji, Ministry of Health, Women and Social Welfare. 2008.

Fiji Islands: A National Policy on Persons Living with Disabilities, 2008–2018. Suva.

Government of Fiji, Ministry of Social Welfare, Women, and Poverty Alleviation. 2014. *Fiji National Gender Policy.* Suva.

Government of Fiji. 2017. *Twenty-Year Development Plan 2017–2036.* Suva.

Government of Samoa, Ministry of Finance. 2021. *Samoa 2040: Transforming Samoa to a Higher Growth Path.* Apia.

Hoddinott, J., H. Alderman, J. R. Behrman, L. Haddad, and S. Horton. 2013. The Economic Rationale for Investing in Stunting Reduction. *Maternal and Child Nutrition* 9 (Suppl 2). pp. 69–82.

International Labour Organization (ILO). 2021. *Innovation to Increase Access to Social Security in Vanuatu.* ILO in the Pacific. 31 August.

Larasati, D., K. Huda, A. Cote, S. K. Rahayu, and M. Siyaranamual. 2019. Inclusive Social Protection for Persons with Disability in Indonesia. *TNP2K Policy Briefs.* January.

Pacific Community (SPC). 2021. *8th Pacific Statistics Methods Board Meeting Summary Report and Outcomes.* Suva.

Pacific Disability Forum. 2018. *Pacific Disability Forum SDG-CRPD Monitoring Report 2018—From Recognition to Realisation of Rights: Furthering Effective Partnership for an Inclusive Pacific 2030.* Suva.

Samson, M., G. Fajth, and D. Francois. 2016. Cognitive Capital, Equity and Child Sensitive Social Protection in Asia and the Pacific. *BMJ Global Health* 1 (Supp 2).

Socialprotection.org. Social Welfare Scheme (accessed 12 May 2022).

United Nations Children Fund (UNICEF). 2018. UN Agencies Raise Alarm over Weakened Fight against Hunger and Malnutrition in Asia and the Pacific. Press release. 2 November.

United Nations Development Programme (UNDP) and UN Women. 2021. *COVID-19 Global Gender Response Tracker.* Version 2 (accessed 12 May 2022)

United Nations Partnership on the Rights of Persons with Disabilities (UNPRPD). 2020. Initial Overview of Specific Social Protection Measures for Persons with Disabilities and Their Families in Response to COVID-19 Crisis. Draft.

Social protection in the Pacific: Historical trends and future pathways for investment

With a need to expand formal social safety nets, this article looks at the history of social protection in the Pacific and how governments can chart a path toward sustainable financing of a core package of social assistance schemes. It does not assess or cost community and indigenous social safety nets, which play a critical and complementary role to government-funded social protection systems across the Pacific.

SNAPSHOT OF GOVERNMENT SOCIAL PROTECTION INVESTMENT IN THE PACIFIC

Government expenditure on social protection[1] is variable across the Pacific and particularly low in some countries (Figure 2). Kiribati spends about 6.3% of gross national income (GNI) while Papua New Guinea (PNG), Solomon Islands, and Vanuatu have no expenditure according to the classification used here. Most countries spend 1% of GNI or less. There is a trend toward investing in core life cycle programs, with universal old age and disability benefits forming most social protection expenditure in the subregion. These core schemes are typical even in high-income countries, where the largest investments across social security and social assistance are the old-age and disability pensions.[2]

Figure 2: Social Protection and Provident Fund Expenditure, Latest Year

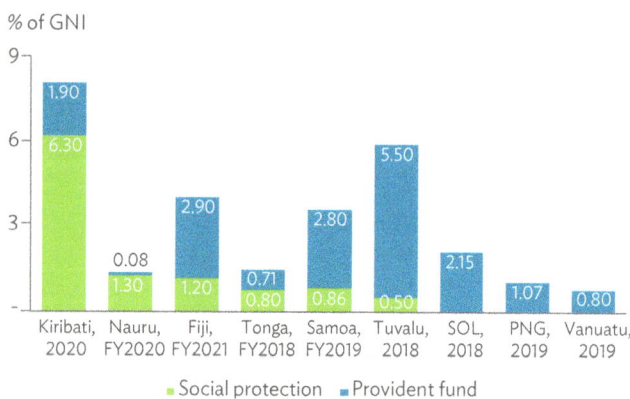

FY = fiscal year, GNI = gross national income, PNG = Papua New Guinea, SOL = Solomon Islands.

Notes:

1. The data follows the classification of social benefits (27) within the economic classification of government expenditure, following the approach described in International Monetary Fund. 2014. *Government Finance Statistics Manual 2014*. Washington, DC. This captures government reporting on social insurance benefits, social assistance benefits, and public service benefits (described as employment-related social benefits in the GFSM 2014). It excludes health care, scholarship programs, school feeding, and labor market programs which, in most cases, are not included under social benefits.

2. Fiscal years end on 30 June for Nauru, Samoa, and Tonga; 31 July for Fiji; and 31 December for other countries included in the chart.

Sources: Authors' calculations using data from national budget documents.

The classification of social protection expenditure in Figure 2 excludes some schemes, which are sometimes discussed as a form of social protection; for example, provident funds. The figure illustrates that payouts from provident funds commonly exceed social protection expenditure in most countries across the Pacific. Despite these high levels of expenditure, these schemes primarily benefit workers in formal employment. The lack of risk pooling among scheme members and the fact that benefits are usually paid as lump sums also limit the level of security provided by such schemes.

Further, Figure 2 presents expenditure data as a percentage of GNI rather than gross domestic product (GDP), which is more common in cross-country comparison of social protection expenditure. This is because many Pacific economies have significant income from items that are not included within GDP, such as remittances, grants, and fees for single-source revenues (e.g., fishing licenses), which means that comparisons to GDP can give a distorted view of levels of expenditure.

As a core government activity, mature social protection systems can absorb large budgets. However, social protection remains a small part of government expenditure in most Pacific countries. Expenditure on social assistance is significantly below the levels of expenditure on health and education in most cases (Figure 3) and much lower than other lower middle-income countries and Organisation for Economic Co-operation and Development countries which have social protection expenditure on average of 14%[3] and 35%, respectively.

Figure 3: Social Assistance Expenditure Compared to Health and Education Expenditure, 2021

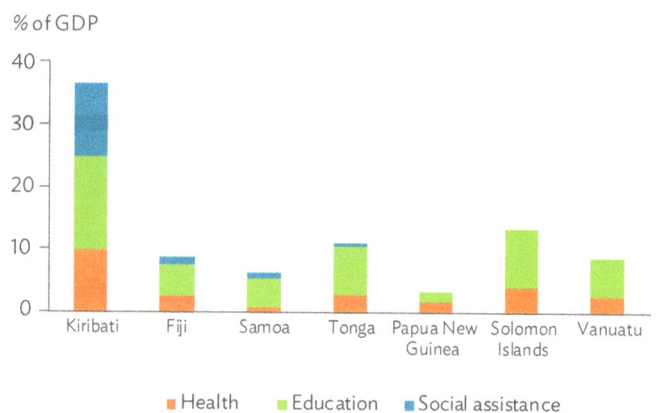

GDP = gross domestic product.

Source: Authors' calculations using national budget documents.

HISTORY OF GOVERNMENT-FUNDED SOCIAL PROTECTION IN THE PACIFIC

Government-funded social protection systems in the Pacific have evolved over the past 5 decades (Figure 4). Up until the late 1980s, most countries only had provident funds in place, usually having been introduced shortly before or after independence. Social assistance schemes are a far newer feature, with almost all having been introduced in the last 15–20 years. Fiji stands out as having a long-standing general social assistance scheme in place that was reformed in 1975,[4] and having introduced a benefit for children (the Care and Protection Allowance) in 1990.

Figure 4: Timeline of Introduction of Main Social Protection Schemes

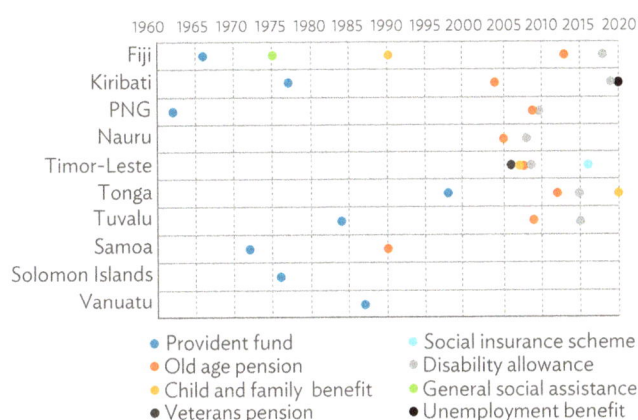

PNG = Papua New Guinea.
Source: Social Protection Approaches to COVID-19: Expert advice helpline internal stocktake on Pacific social protection systems, 2021.

In response to the impacts of the coronavirus disease (COVID-19) pandemic, many Pacific countries utilized social protection measures to cushion increased household hardship, protect jobs, and act as an automatic stabilizer to preserve purchasing power and support aggregate demand within national economies. An analysis funded by Australia's Department of Foreign Affairs and Trade[5] conducted in 2021 found that 13 Pacific island governments had implemented 83 social protection measures since the pandemic began.

Social assistance measures and, within those, cash transfer, accounted for most responses. Countries that had comprehensive responses used multiple social protection measures and different types of social protection programs. Those with existing social assistance programs leveraged routine delivery systems to support their response. Some countries implemented new programs to reach new populations, such as informal workers and the unemployed; and a handful of countries implemented near-universal emergency payments.

Development partners also stepped up their investment in social protection during the pandemic. Australia provided more than A$194 million in grant funding and technical assistance to support

social protection measures, complemented by technical advice to governments to help strengthen social protection national policies, public sector capability, and delivery systems.

Social protection measures have been integral to the Pacific's response to the pandemic, arguably representing a "tipping point" for the sector. But there remain large gaps (particularly for informal sector workers, the unemployed, women, and children), reducing the potential for a broader contribution to economic development. Existing social assistance programs have delivered clear economic dividends. For example, Nauru's social protection programs have reduced poverty by 4.4% according to the national poverty line.[6] Similarly, in Timor-Leste, the elderly pension has reduced national poverty rates from 54% to 49% of the population, and poverty among older persons from 55% to 38%.[7]

Beyond direct poverty reduction, a growing body of evidence internationally points to the critical contribution that adequate social protection systems can play in supporting economic growth when combined with other key social and economic policies. At the household level, social protection systems positively impact key aspects of human capital, including nutrition, health, and education outcomes, while increasing employment and helping to finance productive livelihood activities. At a community level, social protection can stimulate rural economies through local economic multipliers. Social protection has been found to create similar multipliers at the macro level, which can stimulate business activities of actors in the economy. It also provides one of the most direct tools to reduce levels of inequality, which can create a drag on economic growth. Beyond economic arguments, social protection plays a key role in supporting human dignity and social cohesion.

The key question for policymakers is the extent to which countries can create fiscal space for new investments in social protection to provide adequate support along the life cycle and against different types of shocks.

MAKING IT WORK: FINANCING STRATEGIC AND SUSTAINABLE SOCIAL PROTECTION SYSTEMS

Public finances of countries in the Pacific face significant challenges as they emerge from the COVID-19 crisis, especially as they confront growing inflationary pressures. Most of these countries face an immediate challenge to reduce government deficits, and many are considered at moderate or high risk of debt distress. There is significant uncertainty on the economic outlook of the subregion with subsequent downgrades in GDP rebounds and growth.

Options to expand fiscal space will be limited and most countries will need to take an incremental approach to expanding social protection. However, the history of social protection across the subregion provides numerous examples of how this can be achieved, particularly for social assistance. For example, Fiji has increased expenditure on its core social assistance schemes from 0.4% to 1.1% of GDP over a 5-year period, but only with incremental increases in any given year (Figure 5). These have mostly included gradual expansion of eligibility and increases in benefit levels.

Figure 5: Expenditure on Main Social Assistance Schemes in Fiji, 2013–2022

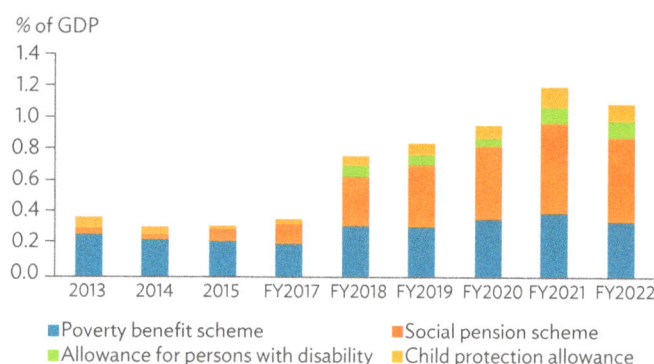

% of GDP

Legend:
- Poverty benefit scheme
- Social pension scheme
- Allowance for persons with disability
- Child protection allowance

FY = fiscal year, GDP = gross domestic product.
Note: In 2016, the Government of Fiji adopted a fiscal year ending 31 July.
Source: Government of Fiji, Ministry of Economy. *Budget Estimates*. Suva (9 years: 2013–2022).

For countries without any government-led systems, the introduction of old age pensions with gradual reductions in the age of eligibility (such as undertaken by Fiji, Kiribati, and Tonga), or child benefits with gradual increases in age of eligibility could be a positive first step. PNG will soon introduce the subregion's first national child benefit focused on the first 1,000 days, with support of the World Bank and the Government of Australia. Timor-Leste is also rolling out a new child grant, starting with 0–3-year-olds and eventually expanding to include school-aged children. Focusing on nonworking-age life-course vulnerabilities can provide significant support to people of all ages, but with reduced concern about creating disincentives for work or about the need for "graduation" or "exit strategies."

Countries can also pursue incremental increases in benefit levels (as Kiribati, Fiji, Tonga, and Samoa have done) by introducing schemes with lower benefit levels and increasing them over time to provide higher levels of adequacy and manage affordability.

It is common for countries to gradually add new schemes to their social protection system over time. One notable trend in the sequencing of schemes in the Pacific has been the introduction of old age pensions, followed later by the introduction of disability benefits. This sequence was followed in Fiji, Kiribati, Nauru, and Tuvalu.

Some countries in the subregion have managed affordability by providing differentiated benefit levels for different categories of beneficiaries. For disability benefits, this involves different benefit levels depending on the severity of disability (as in Kiribati, Palau, Tonga, and Tuvalu). For old age pensions, this usually entails higher benefit levels for older age groups (as in Tonga and Nauru), which arguably acts as a proxy for levels of disability and care needs. Fiji's Care and Protection Allowance differentiates benefits according to level of schooling. On one hand, this approach can be seen as a long-term approach for tailoring adequacy according to the circumstances and support needs of recipients. On the other, it can also be used as a mechanism to contain cost in the short to medium term, keeping benefit levels lower for those with lower support needs.

COSTING A BASIC PACKAGE OF CORE SOCIAL ASSISTANCE IN THE PACIFIC

Australia's Partnerships for Social Protection program (www.p4sp.org) costed a basic package of social assistance schemes for its focus countries in the Pacific. It calculated the cost of three core programs: universal old age pensions, disability benefits, and child benefits for children (0–5 years)[8] at between 0.8% and 2.2% of GDP. The results of the costings are shown in Figure 6 for seven countries based on the assumptions that are detailed in Table 1.

The higher-cost scenario would require about 2.0% of GDP in all countries (between 1.9% of GDP in PNG and 2.2% of GDP in Tonga). The lower-cost package would require about 1.0% of GDP in all countries (between 0.8% in Samoa, and 1.2% in Tonga). Given that benefits are determined as a percentage of GDP per capita, the differences in costs between countries are the result of demographics. Countries such as PNG, Solomon Islands, and Vanuatu are those with relatively smaller older populations, and larger populations of children (hence lower costs for old age pensions and higher costs for child benefits). Countries such as Fiji and Tonga have larger older populations (hence higher old age pension costs).

Importantly, Figure 6 shows that the cost of a basic package of life cycle of social protection is modest in countries across the subregion. For countries not currently investing in social assistance, these levels of expenditure provide a reasonable level of ambition over the medium to long term. For countries already investing in life cycle social protection schemes, the expenditure gap to achieve these basic packages is lower.

Table 1: Assumptions for Basic Social Protection Packages

Scheme	Higher Coverage and Adequacy		Lower Coverage and Adequacy	
	Age of Eligibility	Benefit Level (% of GDP per capita)	Age of Eligibility	Benefit Level (% of GDP per capita)
Child benefit	0–5 years	6	0–5 years	4
Disability benefit	0–64 years	20	0–69 years	10
Old age benefit	65+ years	20	70+ years	10

GDP = gross domestic product.
Source: Partnerships for Social Protection (P4SP).

Figure 6: Cost of Basic Package of Social Protection Benefits (Higher Coverage and Adequacy)

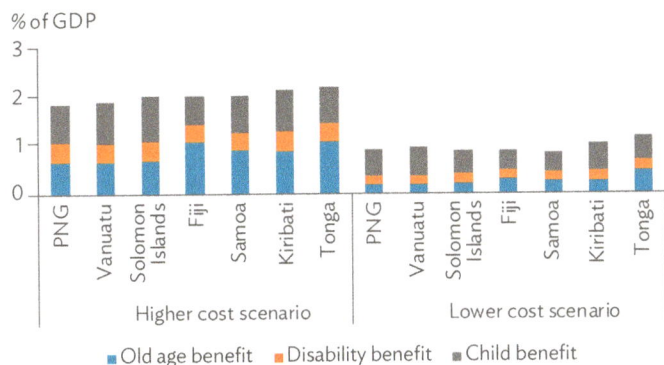

GDP = gross domestic product, PNG = Papua New Guinea.
Source: Partnerships for Social Protection (P4SP) calculations based on data from United Nations, Department of Economic and Social Affairs, Population Division. 2019. World Population Prospects. New York.

Of course, these projections do not estimate the administrative cost and complexities in many of the countries and their varying operational environments (e.g., infrastructure of other public services, banking networks, and mobile phone coverage). These constraints are shared challenges for most sectors of government service delivery, and social protection can play a role in unblocking bottlenecks.

SOCIAL PROTECTION IN THE PACIFIC: THE WAY FORWARD

The compounding impacts of COVID-19, disasters and climate change, and recent cost of living pressures are putting Pacific island households and economies under strain. Some analysts have warned of the risk of a "lost decade of development" and proposed that this can be avoided through productive public investment.[9] Expanding social protection can help address persistent levels of poverty and hardship, stimulate inclusive economic development, and mitigate the impacts of future idiosyncratic and covariate shocks.

Countries across the subregion face difficult choices to ensure the continuity of essential services and investments while optimizing space for recovery and growth. Social protection is an important ingredient in this mix, increasing people's access to the cash needed to meet their basic needs, help them access essential services, and invest in their own future. Zooming out, it can work both to stimulate economic recovery as well as reduce inequality to help counterbalance economic cycles. Further, as a visible and quite direct marker of the state's commitment to its citizens, social protection schemes can help build the social contract. Arguably, it can work to redistribute wealth derived from resource extraction.

Finding the fiscal space for social protection is a challenge, but there are opportunities to do so. Pacific countries have shown the potential to expand social protection systems through incremental investments in life cycle schemes which compound over time. Even in the absence of new funding allocations, there is value in extracting fiscal space for social protection through redirection of inefficient or

ineffective expenditure. Development partners, like Australia and the multilateral banks, can continue to play a critical role supporting Pacific island governments subject to individual partner priorities.

Awareness is growing among governments, including ministries of finance, that increased investments in social protection are needed. The 2022 Pacific Island Forum Economic Ministers Meeting acknowledged the importance of progressing inclusive social protection systems, including through universal social protection measures and strengthening life span social protection schemes. Where identified as a priority by Pacific island governments, Australia stands ready to partner with them so that social protection systems can achieve reductions in poverty and inequality and build community resilience and social cohesion as well as inclusive economic growth.

Lead authors: Charles Knox-Vydmanov, independent consultant; Nikunj Soni, public financial management specialist; Sinta Satriana, social protection specialist, Partnerships for Social Protection; Juliet Attenborough, senior social protection specialist, Partnerships for Social Protection; and Erin Gleeson, assistant director, social protection, Office of the Pacific, Australia's Department of Foreign Affairs and Trade.

Endnotes

1. DFAT defines social protection as consisting of "programs that address risk, vulnerability, inequality and poverty through a system of transfers to people in cash or in kind. The transfers can be funded by contributions from recipients (social insurance) or by government (social assistance)."
2. Australian Institute of Health and Welfare. Welfare expenditure.
3. Manuel, M. 2022. *Financing Social Protection: Domestic and external options in low-income countries.*
4. The Family Assistance Programme was introduced in 1975 as a reform of existing allowances for poor individuals and households that had their origins in the 1920s. These earlier allowances are not included in the timeline, given a lack of information about their specific date of introduction. The Family Assistance Programme was reformed again into the Poverty Benefit Scheme in 2012.
5. Beazley, R. et al. 2021. *Social protection responses to the COVID-19 pandemic in the Pacific: A tipping point for the sector?*
6. Government of Nauru. 2022. *National Social Protection Strategy, 2022–2032.* Yaren.
7. International Labour Organization. 2016. *Universal old-age and disability pensions: Timor-Leste.*
8. It is not completely comprehensive and does not include schemes such as maternity benefits and poverty-targeted social assistance that may still play a complementary role to life cycle schemes.
9. Rajah, R. and A. Dayant. 2020. Avoiding a Pacific Lost Decade: Financing the Pacific's COVID-19 Recovery; *Lowy Institute.* 8 December; and Howes, S. and H. Liu. 2022. The Pacific post-pandemic: an economic update. Presentation prepared for the 2022 Pacific Update Conference. Fiji. 28–30 June.

Social protection at the crossroads: Taking the "high road" toward universal social protection

SETTING THE REGIONAL CONTEXT

Following 2 decades of strong economic growth in Asia and the Pacific, coronavirus disease (COVID-19) struck, sending a powerful reminder of the persistent and structural challenges faced by the region. With many countries not always able to convert economic growth into quality jobs and generate stable incomes, even before the crisis, 930 million workers in the region were working in various forms of vulnerable employment; for example, as own-account or unpaid contributing family workers (ILO 2018). The region is home to 1.3 billion informal workers (representing 68.0% of the total workforce), most of whom work in poor conditions with no or very limited access to social protection[1] (ILO 2020). Gender inequality remains a central characteristic of labor markets, with women receiving lower pay than men and spending more time in unpaid care work.

Despite progress in recent years and the increased attention devoted to social protection in the region, the stark reality is that 55.9% of the population still do not have access to any form of social protection, and only 54.7% of people in the workforce make payments to a contributory scheme.[2] The current crisis has once more exposed the costs of having so large a percentage of the population uncovered by social protection, particularly those working in the informal economy.

Social protection in the region needs to respond not only to the pandemic, but to other major trends as well, including population ageing, migration, urbanization, technological progress, and disasters and climate change (UNESCAP and ILO 2020). Among these, demographic transformations, such as population ageing; changing family structures, including a shift from extended to nuclear families; and migratory flows, place pressure on families and pension systems. The region's vulnerability to climate change and disasters because of natural hazards calls for social protection measures to improve its resilience.

These developments also affect the traditional role of families and communities in social protection provision, adding urgency to the imperative for the establishment of public social protection systems and thereby modifying the debate on the region's future.

Many countries have responded decisively to the COVID-19 pandemic to ensure that people can effectively access health care, while supporting jobs and income security for those most affected.

They have built social protection floors that guarantee a basic level of social security for all as a springboard toward higher levels of formality, productivity, and protection. At the same time, many countries have defended and further expanded higher levels of protection to as many people as possible and are adapting their social security systems to new challenges, guided by the social security standards of the International Labour Organization (ILO).

However, these efforts have so far been held back by insufficient capacities to implement comprehensive national social protection policies on par with economic and employment policies; insufficient fiscal space for social protection exacerbated by fiscal consolidation measures; institutional fragmentation; insufficient involvement of workers' and employers' organizations; and sometimes contradictory policy advice, including by international development partners.

SOCIAL PROTECTION AT THE CROSSROADS

As the World Social Protection Report 2020–2022 and its Regional Companion Report for Asia and the Pacific point out, social protection is at a critical crossroads (ILO 2021 and 2021a). Countries can use the policy window that has been pried open by the pandemic and build on their crisis-response measures to strengthen their social protection systems and progressively close gaps. The ILO advocates for the application of a "high-road" strategy, with a significant new role for social protection, setting out to be inclusive and leaving no one behind, while supporting greater growth, driven by domestic demand, and contributing to further development of human capabilities (Figure 7). The other option is to focus on fiscal consolidation and pursue a "low-road" approach that continues the pattern of underdeveloped social protection systems and could keep countries trapped in a "low cost–low human development" growth pattern.

Considering the nature of the reforms required, social dialogue needs to be at the core of the process, with strong participation by social partners ensuring the involvement of both those contributing to and those benefiting from the system. Meaningful and effective participation by workers, employers, and other stakeholders not only helps ensure that social protection policies respond to people's needs; it is also key to building trust, public support, and a sense of ownership, thereby facilitating the implementation of policies.

Up to now, social protection has been, for many countries in the region, a residual element of public policy, mostly limited to supporting the most vulnerable rather than a developmental tool to enhance both economic development and resilience. Only if it is recognized as an integral part of a renewed socioeconomic model can social protection achieve the policy and fiscal space it needs to have a transformational impact in societies.

Equally, by occupying a more central space in public policy, enhanced social protection can support the social contract and generate public trust in the state, with a positive impact on social cohesion. The provision of more inclusive and adequate social protection can also contribute to building human capabilities and enhance productivity, thereby creating conditions for the generation of increased government resources, through both taxation and social security contributions, and enlarging the fiscal space for redistribution. Without this positive transformation and an overall increase in the fiscal resources allocated to social protection, the objective of universal social protection will remain unachievable for most of the countries in the region.

Figure 7: Social Protection at the Crossroads

Source: International Labour Organization. 2021. *World Social Protection Report 2020–22: Social protection at the crossroads – in pursuit of a better future.*

Today's transformations require new adaptations of social protection systems to ensure that they can continue to play their protective role for workers already covered and expand to cover additional workers, while facilitating the transformation of economies and societies and creating a bridge toward a future that works for all.

High levels of informality require a context-specific mix of traditional and novel approaches to ensure that all workers have access to social protection. Linking different policy areas, and strengthening synergies between them, can generate multiple positive spin-offs. For example, linking social security institutions with tax authorities—as was done for pensions in Japan, Mongolia, and the People's Republic of China; and social health protection in Indonesia, the Philippines, and Viet Nam—would have the potential to generate new ways to extend coverage. At the same time, linking training and skills-upgrading programs with social protection can help develop the productivity of workers and enhance their employability (ILO 2019).

Enterprise formalization is another important step toward extension of contributory coverage. The costs of formalization can represent, particularly for micro and small enterprises, a disincentive to move toward formal arrangements. A successful strategy for formalization should take into account these considerations and develop a full package of incentives as part of a comprehensive strategy that could include support to increase productivity, access to credit and simplified tax and contributions assessments, as well as access to social security coverage, potentially facilitated by digital technologies.

Realizing the important role of social protection as a social and economic stabilizer, countries should seize this opportunity to make the human right[3] to social security a reality for all. Recovery will only be sustained, and future crises mitigated if countries move toward comprehensive, sustainable, and shock-responsive social protection systems. Social protection policies that enable people to better navigate life and work transitions, structural changes in the labor market, and systemic shocks respond better to the ILO's Centenary Declaration's call for a human-centered future of work,[4] and contribute to the achievement of the United Nations' 2030 Agenda for Sustainable Development.

THE COSTS OF NO SOCIAL PROTECTION

Social protection is a human right to which everyone in any society should have access; it is also a prerequisite for social cohesion and justice. It constitutes a powerful tool to alleviate poverty and inequality, as demonstrated through long experience in more developed countries, as well as in Organisation for Economic Co-operation and Development countries that invested early in social development.

The costs and impact of neglecting social protection are borne by society as a whole at different levels, including the state, communities, the voluntary sector, families, enterprises, and individual citizens. There are several sets of costs and impacts that result from neglect or abandonment of social protection.

The first set relates to poverty and vulnerability since there is a clear positive correlation between these and weak or non-existent social protection. These are huge costs since they not only lead to people being chronically socially excluded, but also to people being dissatisfied and disaffected by society. Impoverished populations not only suffer from exclusion from essential goods, services, and rights, but also suffer the loss of potential for individual development and to contribute positively to collective development in the social, political, and cultural fields.

A second set of costs relates to the economy. If there is a situation where many people are unemployed or living in poverty, then this is a productive loss to the economy. Further, without social protection or any means of support, wage demands will rise (a cost that must be met by the employers and/or the state). There is also the fact that cutbacks in social and health services can lead to greater costs for the state in the long term.

A third set is the cost to human capital. A lack of investment in public benefits and services means a decrease in life expectancy, health, education, and skills, and a lack of investment in the younger generation. Hence, the current and future stock of a country's human capital is diminished.

Fourth, there are costs in terms of the reduction of political capital. Neglecting or abandoning social protection reduces the legitimacy of the state.

For all the above, no country or indeed region can afford to neglect or undermine social protection at any level, and that particularly integrated, transparent, deliberate, and participatory approaches should be encouraged. Effective access to social protection is not a luxury and should be perceived as an investment in people, social justice, and social cohesion, with a high rate of return not only in economic terms but also in social and environmental terms, and as constituting an indispensable and solid foundation for sustainable and peaceful development for all. In this sense, social protection can be considered as an investment and, consequently, as a productive factor. Poor countries need to invest in social protection if they want to break the vicious circles of poverty and underdevelopment and begin to contribute positively to local, national, regional, and global development.

CONCLUSIONS AND POSSIBLE WAYS FORWARD

A human-centered approach to the future of work calls for universal access to comprehensive, adapted, and sustainable social protection systems that provide benefits for all, during the entire life course, and in response to covariate shocks.

Only 8 years remain to achieve the 2030 Agenda, including Sustainable Development Goal target 1.3 on social protection floors.

In a world where the majority of the population has no, or insufficient, access to social protection and is locked in a vicious cycle of vulnerability, poverty, and social exclusion, it is imperative for governments globally to step up their efforts to make the right to social security a reality for all. Today, societies at large are faced with profound transformations. In tandem with the other main public policies, social protection is a lubricant of change, and investments made in social protection help navigate life and work transitions and structural change, and protect workers and enterprises. In this context, it is crucial to adapt national social protection policies and systems to the new global realities, uphold and enhance their protective function, and support these transformations. Achieving these objectives by 2030 requires strong political will and social dialogue, translated into effective policies and corresponding implementation strategies, comprehensive legal frameworks, and sustainable financing mechanisms.

The COVID-19 pandemic has underscored the need for stronger social protection systems. This means that the temporary measures adopted in this crisis to close coverage gaps are utilized as building blocks for establishing rights-based national social protection systems.

Lead author: Markus Ruck, social protection specialist, International Labour Organization Decent Work Technical Support Team for East and South East Asia and the Pacific.

Endnotes

[1]   The concepts of "social security" and "social protection" are used interchangeably in this article, and cover all measures that provide benefits through contributory or noncontributory mechanisms (or a mix thereof), whether in cash or in kind, to realize the human right to social security and to secure protection, inter alia, from (i) lack of work-related income (or insufficient income) resulting from sickness, disability, maternity, employment injury, unemployment, old age, or death of a family member; (ii) lack of access, or unaffordable access, to health care; (iii) insufficient family support, particularly for children and adult dependents; and (iv) general poverty and social exclusion.

[2]   Data on effective coverage presented in this article come from the following sources: ILO, World Social Protection Database, based on the Social Security Inquiry (accessed October 2022); ILOSTAT (accessed October 2022); and national sources.

[3]   As enshrined in the Universal Declaration of Human Rights (Articles 22 and 25) and the International Covenant on Civil and Political Rights (Articles 9, 11, and 12).

[4]   The ILO Centenary Declaration for the Future of Work (2019) called on member states to develop and enhance social protection systems that are "adequate, sustainable and adapted to developments in the world of work" (II.A.xv); and to strengthen the capacities of all people to benefit from the opportunities of a changing world of work through "universal access to comprehensive and sustainable social protection" (III.A.iii).

References

International Labour Organization (ILO). 2018. *Women and Men in the Informal Economy: A Statistical Picture*, 3rd ed.

ILO. 2019. *Extending social security to workers in the informal economy: Lessons from international experience.*

ILO. 2020. *Asia–Pacific Employment and Social Outlook 2020: Navigating the crisis towards a human-centred future of work.*

ILO. 2021. *World Social Protection Report 2020–22: Social protection at the crossroads – in pursuit of a better future.*

ILO. 2021a. *World Social Protection Report 2020–22: Regional Companion Report for Asia and the Pacific.*

United Nations Economic and Social Commission for Asia and the Pacific (UNESCAP) and ILO. 2020. *The Protection We Want: Social Outlook for Asia and the Pacific.*

Nonfuel Merchandise Exports from Australia
(A$; y-o-y % change, 3-month m.a.)

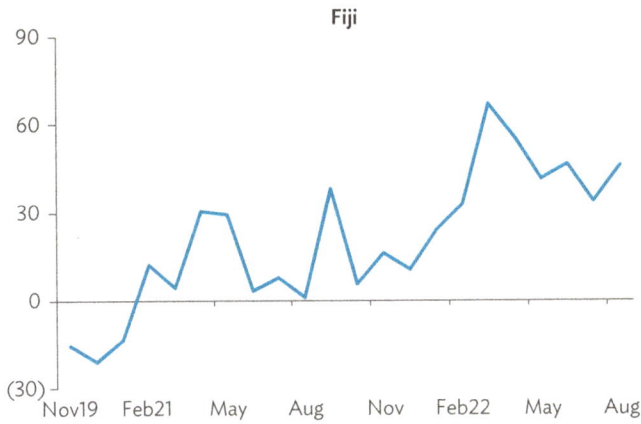

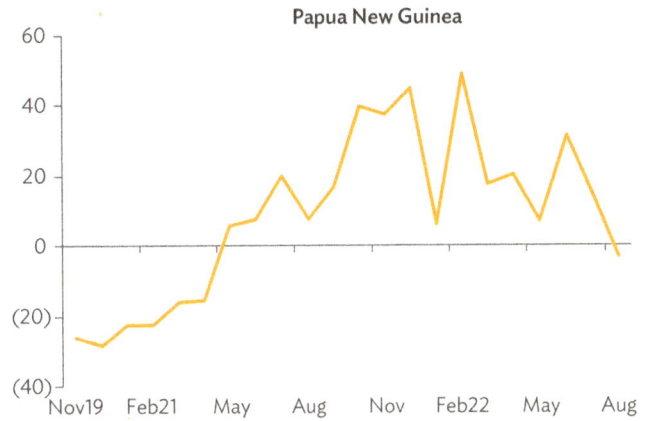

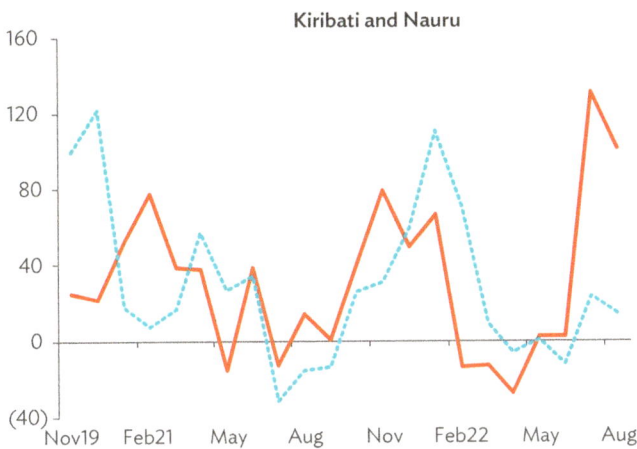

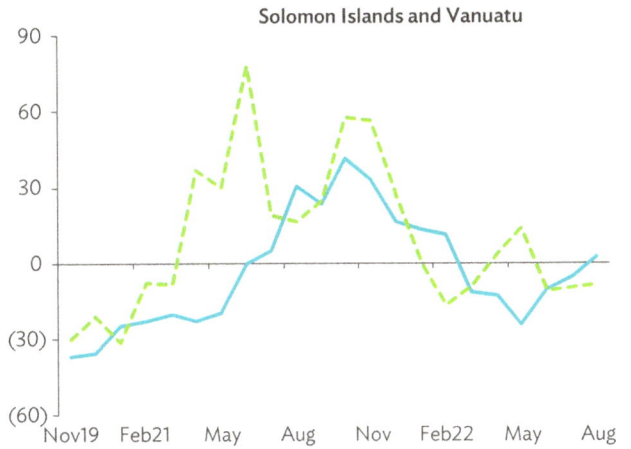

Fiji

Papua New Guinea

Kiribati and Nauru

Kiribati —— Nauru ------

Solomon Islands and Vanuatu

Solomon Islands —— Vanuatu ------

( ) = negative, A$ = Australian dollar, m.a. = moving average, y-o-y = year-on-year.
Source: Australian Bureau of Statistics.

Nonfuel Merchandise Exports from New Zealand and the United States
(y-o-y % change, 3-month m.a.)

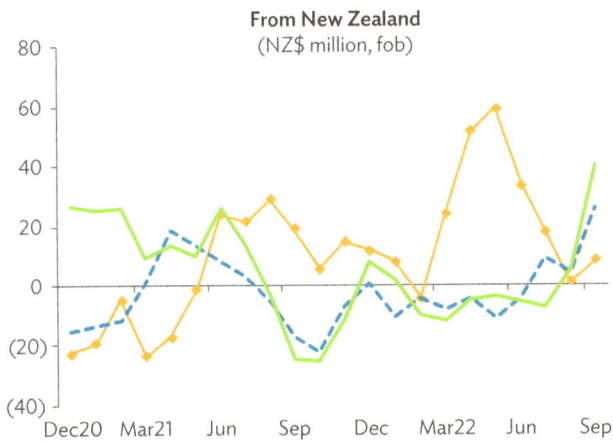

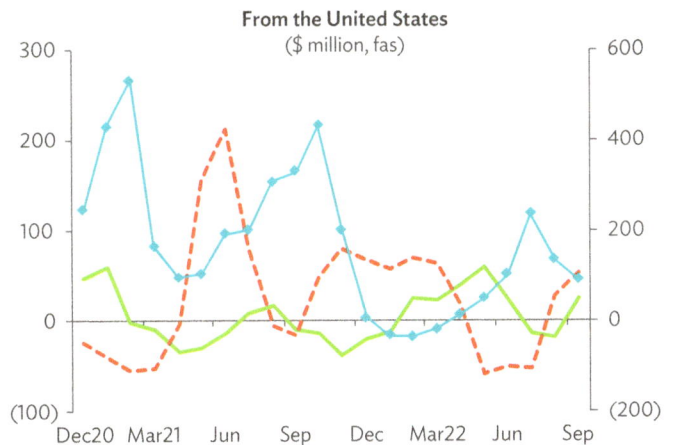

From New Zealand
(NZ$ million, fob)

Cook Islands —— Samoa ------ Tonga ——

From the United States
($ million, fas)

FSM —— RMI (rhs) —— Palau ------

( ) = negative, fas = free alongside, fob = free on board, FSM = Federated States of Micronesia, m.a. = moving average, NZ$ = New Zealand dollar, rhs = right-hand scale, RMI = Republic of the Marshall Islands, y-o-y = year on year.

Sources: Statistics New Zealand and United States Census Bureau.

Diesel Exports from Singapore
(y-o-y % change, 3-month m.a.)

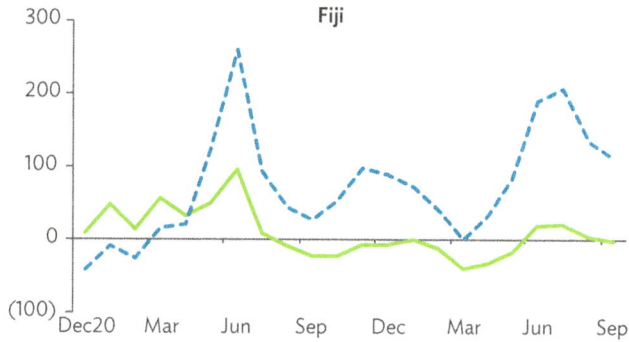

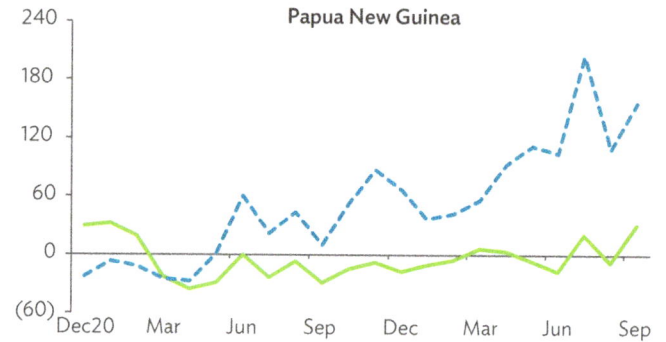

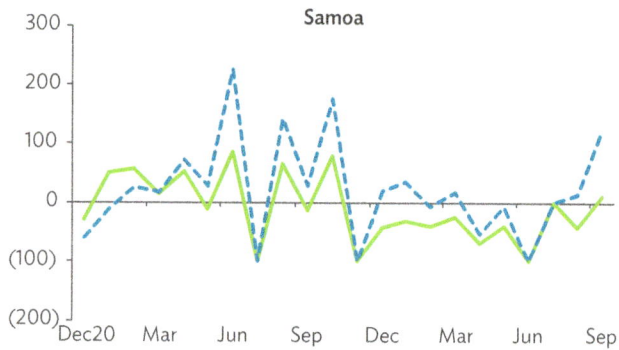

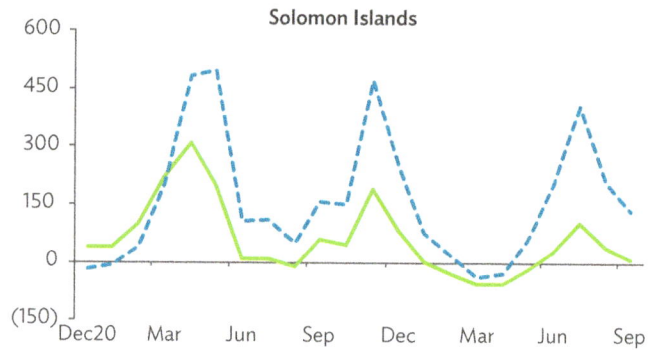

Fiji

Papua New Guinea

Samoa

Solomon Islands

—— Volumes   - - - Values

( ) = negative, m.a. = moving average, y-o-y = year on year.
Source: International Enterprise Singapore.

Gasoline Exports from Singapore
(y-o-y % change, 3-month m.a.)

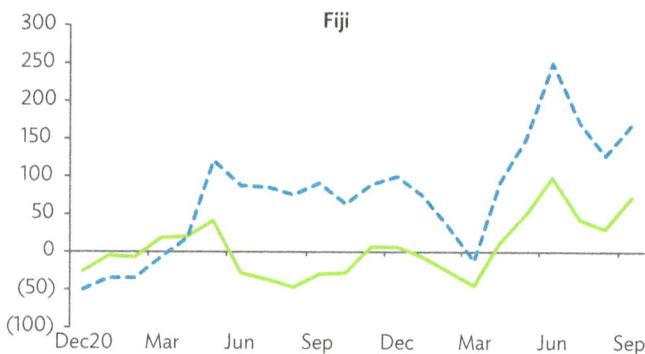

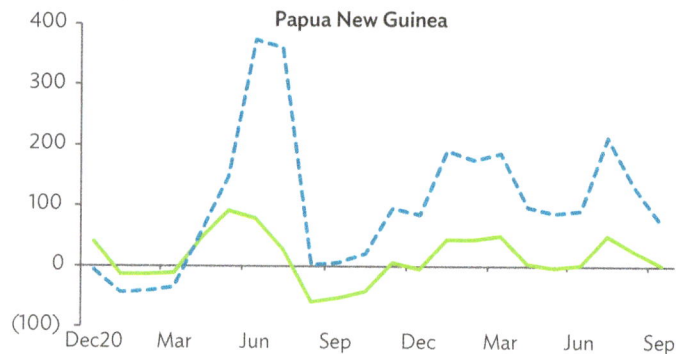

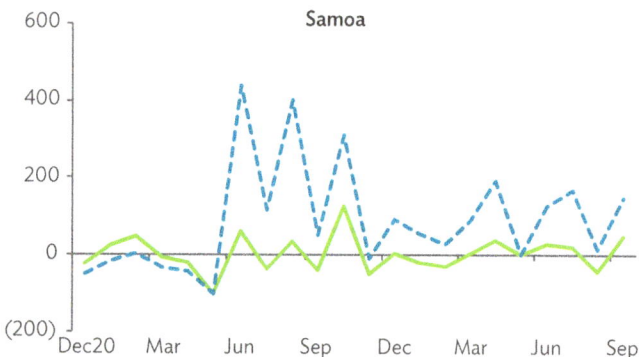

Fiji

Papua New Guinea

Samoa

Solomon Islands

—— Volumes   - - - Values

( ) = negative, m.a. = moving average, y-o-y = year on year.
Source: International Enterprise Singapore.

Departures from Australia to the Pacific
(monthly)

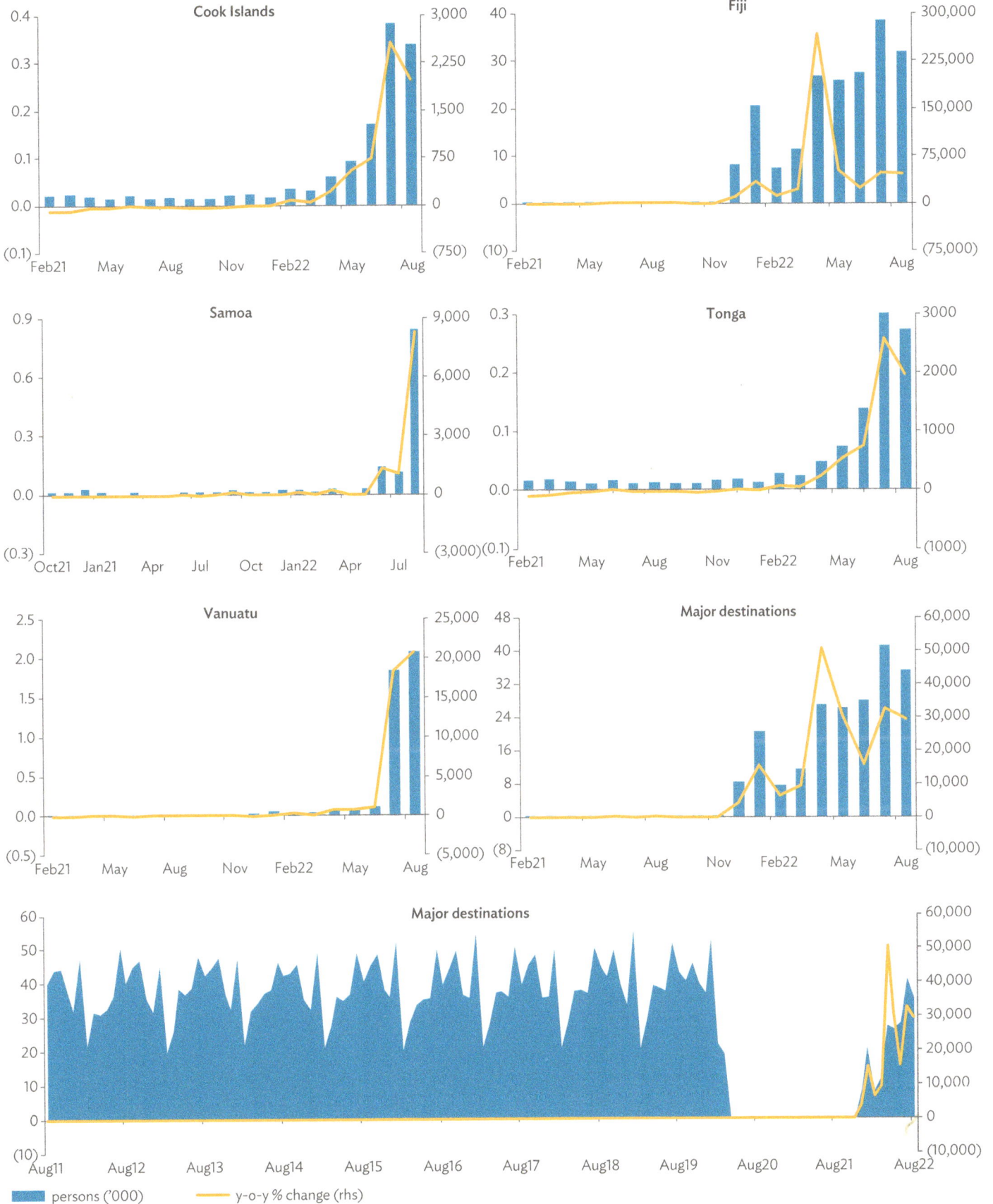

Cook Islands

Fiji

Samoa

Tonga

Vanuatu

Major destinations

Major destinations

■ persons ('000)   ─── y-o-y % change (rhs)

( ) = negative, rhs = right-hand scale, y-o-y = year on year.

Source: Australian Bureau of Statistics.

Departures from New Zealand to the Pacific
(monthly)

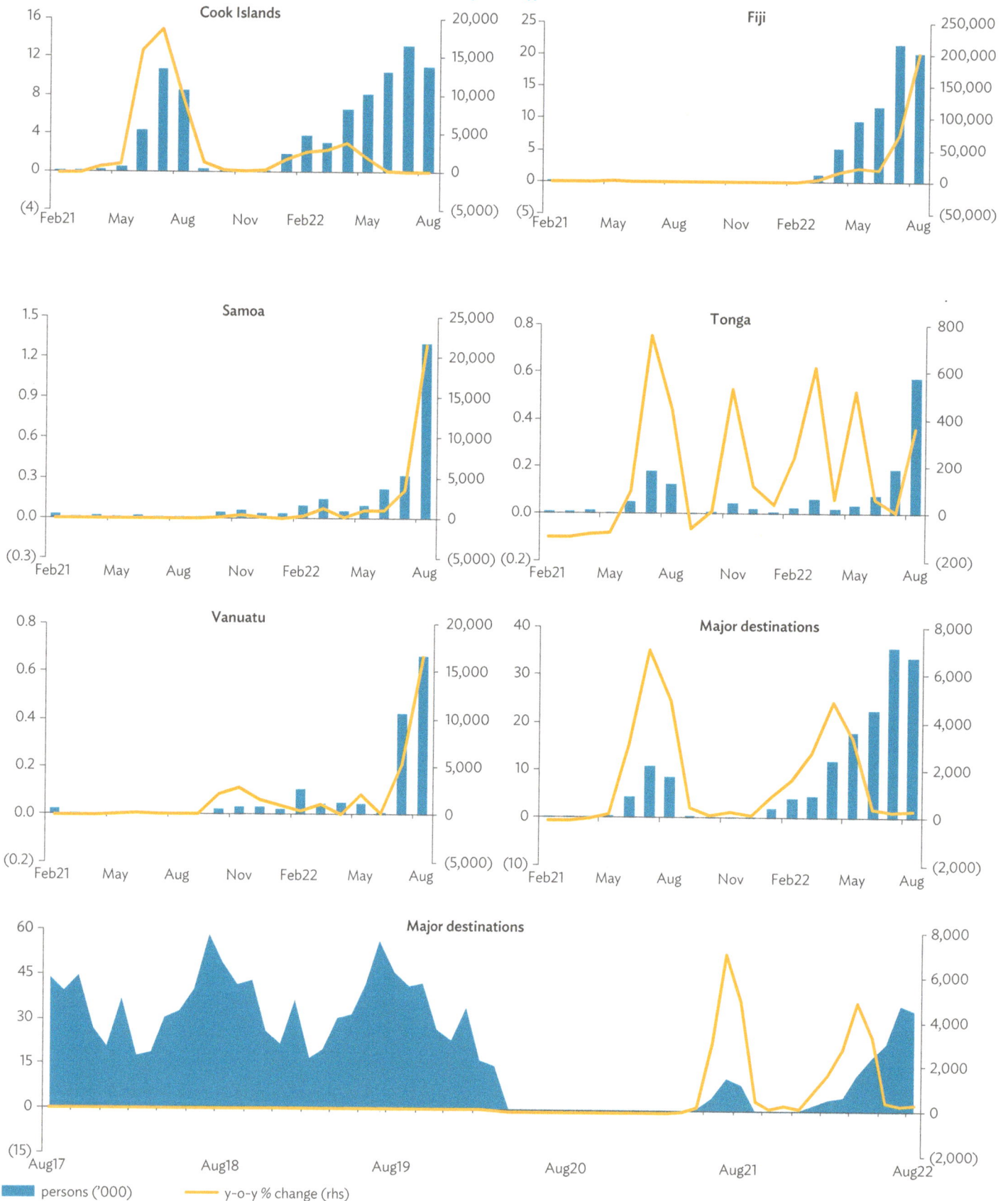

Cook Islands

Fiji

Samoa

Tonga

Vanuatu

Major destinations

Major destinations

■ persons ('000)   —— y-o-y % change (rhs)

( ) = negative, rhs = right-hand scale, y-o-y = year-on-year.
Source: Statistics New Zealand.

www.ingramcontent.com/pod-product-compliance
Lightning Source LLC
Chambersburg PA
CBHW041122280326
41928CB00061B/3500